UNDER THE NEEDWOOD TREE

A glimpse into the History of Barton-under-Needwood

Written and compiled by
STEVE GARDNER

Published by
Barton-under-Needwood Parish Council
Centenary Book Committee 1995

Distributed by
H & H Spalding (Books)
60 Main Street
Barton-under-Needwood
Staffordshire
Tel: (01283) 712220

ISBN 0 9525514 0 3 (paperback edition)
ISBN 0 9525514 1 1 (hardback edition)

Printed by
J. M. Tatler & Son Ltd.
Abbey Street Works, Derby

Front Cover:
A lithograph of Barton-under-Needwood Church, 1860

Back Cover:
The 'Shoulder of Mutton' Inn, Main Street

Contents

Preface	. . . .	i
Barton-under-Needwood Parish Council Coat of Arms	. . . .	ii
List of photographs, illustrations and maps	. . . .	iii
Chapter One	EARLY HISTORY.	1
Chapter Two	FOUR NOTABLE ANCESTORS FROM EARLY HISTORY. . . . . Richard de Holland John Taylor Thomas Russell William Key	10
Chapter Three	BARTON IN THE 18TH AND 19TH CENTURIES	25
Chapter Four	ALL OUR YESTERYEARS . . . . A compilation of news clippings from Dr. Palmer's scrapbook	38
Chapter Five	MEMORIES OF BARTON . . . . with old photographs	49
Chapter Six	THE EVOLUTION OF LOCAL GOVERNMENT	90
Chapter Seven	THE PARISH COUNCILS OF 1894/95 AND 1994/95 . . . . . including the list of councils throughout	93
Chaper Eight	BARTON TODAY.	109
Chapter Nine	A WALK AROUND BARTON	113
Postscript	. . . .	123
Bibliography	. . . .	124

Preface

THERE is no modern history of Barton-under-Needwood, this book has been compiled to give an insight into the history of the village. Stebbing Shaw's *History and Antiquities of Staffordshire* was published long ago in 1798 and includes one chapter on the village, the only other accounts are brief entries in 19th century directories and a few special subject studies. The book contains a summary of what has been published and has attempted no research on primary sources for the early history, in general it aims to provide a background outline history and is published to celebrate the centenary of the Barton Parish Council. The title *Under the Needwood Tree* is one that has been used for some time by the church magazine, *The Barton Chime*. They admit to having borrowed it from Thomas Hardy's famous novel *Under the Greenwood Tree*.

The text of the book has been researched, written and compiled by Steve Gardner together with a sub-committee of the Centenary committee, set up by the Barton Parish Council and the Barton Civic Society. The idea to publish such a book as a part of the centenary celebrations was first suggested by Arthur Kennedy in 1992, but it was 1994 before work got underway, and Steve Gardner offered his services.

Members of the Centenary Book Committee were Arthur Kennedy, Jeff Pattison and Bill Shingles of the Barton Parish Council, who are also members of the Civic Society, and Pauline Shingles and Christine Kennedy of the Civic Society. Arthur and Christine Kennedy produced the sections on the Parish Council's history, and the "Walk around the Village". Jeff Pattison, Chairman of the Centenary Committee, researched and produced the sections on William Key, "The Evolution of Local Government", and "Barton of Today". He also assisted in the research of the "Early History" section. Pauline and Bill Shingles did the research and produced the section on "All Our Yesteryears", the newspaper clippings from the turn-of-the-century scrapbook of Dr. Palmer.

Steve Gardner researched "Early History", Richard de Holland, and the Holland family. John Taylor, "Barton in the 18th and 19th centuries", and the enchanting "Memories of Barton", where some of the village's oldest living parishioners were interviewed.

A special mention must go to Mr. Gerald Carey, an authority on the life and works of Thomas Russell, who prepared the section on Thomas Russell, also to Mrs. Alison Wood and Mr. Graham Joiner, for their advice and assistance. Photographs in the book are from Steve Gardner's private collection, and others loaned from Mrs. N. Upton, Mrs. D. Osbourne, Mrs. M. Johnson, Mrs. F. Scarratt, Mrs. B. Tovey, Mrs. P. Lamley, Mrs. C. Atkin, Mrs. M. Swire, and Mr. K. Garrison. This opportunity is taken to thank them very much for their co-operation. The photographic work was done by Peter Poole and he would be happy to supply copies of any of the pictures in the book. (Tel. no. 01283 762813). Thanks must also go to the people that gave the interviews with Steve for the "memories" section: Mr. J. Hoult, Mrs. J. Haime, Mrs. M. Reeves, Mr. C. Shepherd, Mrs. D. Osbourne, Mrs. M. Shilton, Mrs. G. Price, Mrs. M. Johnson, Mrs. P. Lamley, Mr. A. Reeves, Mrs. F. Scarratt, Mr. D. Swinfield, Mrs. B. Tovey, Mrs. J. Berry, Mrs. K. Mycock, Mrs. N. Upton and Mr. S. Archer who provided information on the late Miss Prior. The help of all of these people is much appreciated, including Mr. L. Blacknell who assisted in the final preparations of the material, and Mr. A. Campion for artwork.

STEVE GARDNER

Barton-under-Needwood Parish Council Coat of Arms

THE coat of arms was adopted by Barton-under-Needwood Parish Council in 1990 after holding a competition among the residents. The design is based on the winning entry by Colin Shingles, formerly a pupil at the John Taylor High School; quadrants have been transposed to make it heraldically correct and balanced. The coat of arms has not been registered with the College of Arms, but is used as a letterhead on the Parish Council stationery and not for commercial profit. The Centenary Committee, made up of Parish Council and Civic Society members, had the design made into a Chairman's Badge of Office. The Civic Society donated £150 towards the purchase price of £433.

The Badge of Office was presented to the Parish Council Chairman, Arthur Kennedy, at the Centenary Dance on 31st December 1994 by the Chairman of the Centenary Committee, Jeff Pattison.

Three Gules (red) Tudor roses on Or (gold) background — symbolising the meeting between Henry VII and the Taylor triplets. One, John Taylor, built St. James' Church and was Master of the Rolls to Henry VIII.

An Argent (silver) Key on Azure (blue) background — symbolising William Key who died in 1651, one of the many benefactors of the poor of Barton, whose charity is still in existence.

An Oak Tree, Vert (green) leaves and Sable (black) trunk on Azure (blue) background — symbolising the Forest of Needwood under which Barton lies in the vale of Trent, and gives the affix to its name.

Three Or (gold) Wheatsheaves on Vert (green) background — symbolising the agricultural industry of Barton and the derivation of its name, Anglo-Saxon for grain field.

List of photographs, illustrations and maps

A lithograph of Barton Church 1860 . . . . *front cover*
Barton-under-Needwood Parish Council Coat of Arms ii
How to find Barton-under-Needwood . . . . *v*
Robert Plots map of Staffordshire 1682, showing Barton and the Needwood Forest 9
Locations map, in and around Barton-under-Needwood 24
The Cottage Hospital, Short Lane 53
Main Street, looking West 53
The Barton Free School, Station Road 54
Mr. Simmonds outside his Barber's shop in Main Street 54
Barton Fire Service 1897, Crew and horse-drawn Engine 59
The Hackett Brothers 59
The Old Workhouse, Wales Lane 60
'Upper' Main Street, looking West 60
Barton Gate, looking towards the 'Top Bell' 65
A postman in Main Street 65
Mr. Scarratt Snr. at his Saddlery shop 66
Alty Scarratt dressed as a nurse at an event in Barton 66
Main Street, looking East 71
Goodwin's shop, Main Street 71
A Barton Cricket Club tea, circa 1920 72
A cottage on 'The Green' 72
'Rest of the Village' cricket team 1895 75
Scorecard for Whites and Palmers versus Rest of the Village 75
Cottages at 'The Efflinch' 76
Mrs. Simmonds outside 'The Victoria Stores' 76
The Wharfhouse, Barton Turns 83
The 'Flitch of Bacon', Catholme Lane 83
Haydon's Shop, Main Street 84
Station Road, looking West 84
Mr. Prior's Upholstery shop, Main Street 87
Horse-drawn cab at the 'Shoulder of Mutton' 87
Barton and Walton Railway Station 88
'Utter Hill', Main Street 88
Francis William Hardy (1855-1950) 97
Rev. William Henry Hutchinson Fairclough 97
Francis John Hardy (1900-1960), Barton Parish Council 98
The Centenary Book Committee of 1995 98
Barton-under-Needwood, places of interest 112
Barton Hall, Dunstall Road 117
Nuttall House, Dunstall Road 117
Silverhill, off Barton Gate 118
Wales End Farm, Wales Lane 118
The 'Shoulder of Mutton' Inn, Main Street . . . . *back cover*

How to Find Barton-under-Needwood

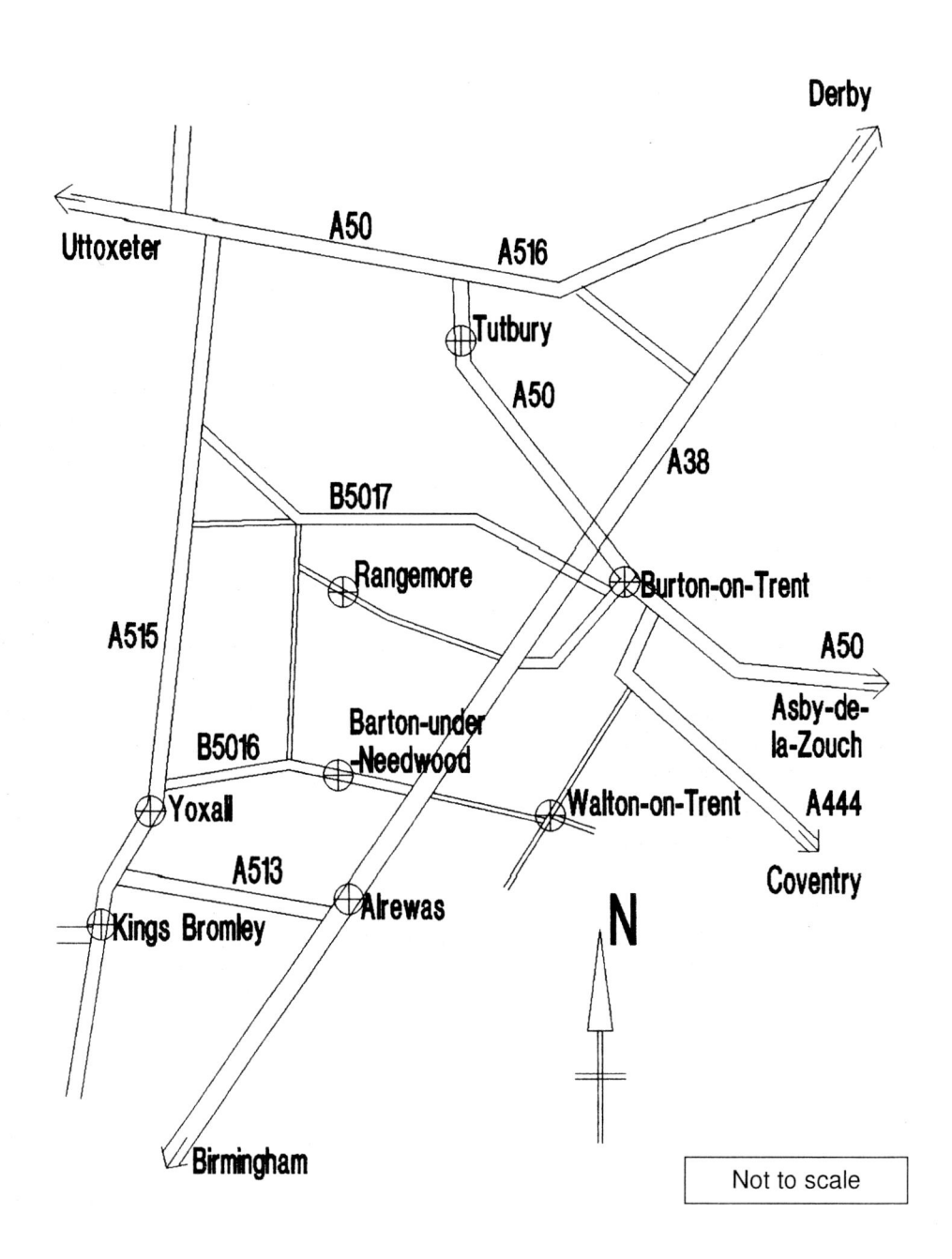

Chapter One
EARLY HISTORY

THERE are few counties in England that are as rich in scenery, architecture and history as Staffordshire. For the most part rural, a county of villages, country inns, historic houses and spectacular countryside, it is rich in industrial heritage which is kept alive today by working museums. One of Staffordshire's villages is Barton-under-Needwood. It was originally a small farming community, which grew, into a large village with a population today of approximately 5,000.

Barton is situated in the vale of the River Trent on the eastern boundary of Staffordshire, it lies 119 miles (192km) from London, approximately 25 miles (40km) north east of Birmingham and 15 miles (24km) south west of Derby. The village is situated on slightly rising ground (175-225 feet above sea level) on the western side of the Trent and a little over a mile from the river. Much of the parish lies in the shallow valley of the brook, a tributary of the Trent, which rises just north of the Yoxall road between Barton Gate and Bar Lane and flows east-south-east through the heart of the village. The brook has made a narrow strip of alluvium on each side of its course, but most of Barton village is situated on the fluvioglacial gravels which were deposited by meltwater at the close of the Ice Age. Deciduous forest would have been the natural vegetation cover.

Little is known of the early history of Barton-under-Needwood. The gravel terraces of the Trent valley contain remnants of prehistoric times, particularly henges, barrows and crop marks. The Trent valley, provided a natural routeway for migrating peoples as well as for trading and military purposes. Invading armies usually followed valleys, and the Romans, the Saxons, the Norsemen and the Normans all passed this way. The Iron Age fort at Borough Hill, Walton, could be considered evidence of the need to control the passage of hostile warriors along the valley.

The fort at Borough Hill was occupied originally by the Coritani tribe, Celtic Brythons, in the period 700-600 BC. The Coritani were tall people with blue eyes and fair hair, and were sun-worshippers who made human sacrifice; they controlled all the

Early History

movement along the then navigable Trent. The Roman road, Ryknield Street, which was possibly a pre-Roman track and adapted by the Romans, is the oldest historical monument in the parish. The road was built to run from Gloucester to Derby via Wall (the Roman city of Letocetum which lies south of Lichfield). The A38 follows much of the line of the former Ryknield Street. The road may have flooded on occasions, but for the most part it lay above the flood plain. The valley provided ease of movement and avoided the denser forest to the west. It is possible that there was a Roman settlement in Barton at around the time of the Roman invasion by Caesar (54 BC). Some Roman artifacts were found in the late 1980s, during the renovation of the Old Parsonage site in the village, near to St. James' church. Aerial photographs have revealed what is thought to be the site of a Roman settlement south of the present Catholme Lane, just east of the railway line.

Stebbing Shaw's *History of Staffordshire*, 1798, describes how, in 1783, some men digging near a pool in a field a little south of Barton's infant school (Russell's Free School as it was known) discovered five Roman urns, lying due east and west. Some contained human bones but they were broken into pieces by careless workmen and were eventually thrown into the pool.

On the north side of Catholme Lane a substantial Anglo-Saxon settlement was found and excavated between 1973 and 1976. This was archaeological evidence of nearly 2.3 hectares of settlement, revealing ground plans of 66 timber buildings, probably representing the development of 5, 6 or 7 holdings or farmsteads existing between the fifth and tenth centuries. The topography at Catholme encouraged settlement, survival and development. It was positioned on the northern end of a slight gravel terrace directly overlooking the River Trent. Its raised position assured against flooding, while the natural benefits of a riverside environment were readily available. The name "Catholme" is Danish "holme" meaning land surrounded by water. In the area of Catholme we can still find other names in existence such as "Fatholme" and "Tucclesholme". The settlement consisted of groups of buildings, enclosed by ditches and connected by trackways. The dating of Catholme came from charcoal samples, using calibration of tree ring chronology. The four earliest dates overlap between the years 450 and 510, while the latest three dates overlap between 890 and 950.

The name 'Barton' is Saxon, and comes from Bertone, which means grainfield, barley store or rickyard. 'Ber' means 'grain' and 'ton' means field or store. The "Under Needwood" was a medieval addition, to distinguish it from other places known as Bertone. It was officially adopted in 1377, but it was first recorded on a deed of 1280.

The forest's name could derive from the Welsh word "nedd" which was a dingle or hollow in the wood, but 'Needwood' is also described as a refuge for outlaws.

Under the Needwood Tree

Barton was in the heart of the kingdom of Mercia, an old English kingdom whose rulers became over-king or bretwalda of the English and Celtic kingdoms in the eighth century. The Anglo-Saxon shire was simply a geographical and administrative area; it had come into existence in Wessex by the tenth century. The shire reeve (hence sheriff), was a royal official. The shire was divided into smaller units known as the hundreds. Staffordshire's hundreds are Pirehill, Totmonslow, Offlow, Cuttlestone and Seisdon. Barton-under-Needwood lies in the hundred of Offlow.

Barton is mentioned in the Old English charter of 942, where King Edmund granted to Wulsige the black lands on the Trent Valley area. This gave him wide possessions including Rothulfston (Rolleston), Alrewasse, Walltune (Walton), Barton, Tatenhyll, Brantiston (Branston), Draca Hlowe (Drakelow), Cotuhalfne (Coton) and Crokeshalle (Croxall).

In the tenth century the settlement at Catholme was abandoned and re-established as Barton a mile and a quarter away. The settlement was possibly exposed to the invading Vikings, but its new location was a better defensive position. Its actual site seems to have been determined by the meeting of two routes, the first being the dry route, valley side from Tatenhill to Wychnor, and the second being the cross valley route from Walton which crossed the river by ford, and on towards Yoxall. In those early years a Saxon church made of wood stood somewhere near to the present-day church in Barton.

By AD 1004 Wulsige's lands in the district had passed into the hands of Wulfric Spot, who was a king's thegn and Earl of Mercia, he was also founder of Burton Abbey. By 1066 Barton was one of the lordships belonging to Earl Algar, son of Leofric and Godiva, who had a large estate in this part of the country, which he left to Edwin his eldest son. On Edwin's rebellion the lands were forfeited to William the Conqueror.

An early official record of Barton is an entry in the Domesday Book, a record of the survey of England in 1086, for William the Conqueror. The Domesday Book records that the king held Barton's 360 acres. The Domesday Book entry for Barton under Needwood, reads;

Terra Regis in OFFELAV HVND
Rex ten Bertone. Algar tennuit. Ibi funt.
111 hidae cu append. Tra. e. XVIII. car. In
Dnio funt. II car. 7. II ferui 7. XVII. uill
7. VIII bord cu. IX car. Ibi. XX. ac pti.
Silua nt. II lecuu lg. 7 una lat. Ibi
molin de. VI. lib. modo. VII. lib

Early History

Translated;
>Land of the king in Offlow hundred
>The king (William 1) holds Barton, earl Algar held it.
>3 hides with its dependencies. (a hide was 120 acres)
>Land for 18 ploughs (a plough team was 8 oxen)
>In demesne (lordship) there are 2 ploughs, 2 slaves, 17 villagers
>8 bordars (smallholders) with 9 ploughs. 20 acres of meadow
>Woodland 2 leagues long and one wide
>There is a mill at 6 shillings. (this value is the annual rent paid to the manor.)
>Tempore Regis Edward, in the time of king Edward (the Confessor),
>that is before 1066, value was £6, now it is £7.
>(these values were the total annual receipts paid to the manor).

The mill referred to was a water-driven mill, down by the river; in 1290 it was recorded as being used in the manufacture of woollens, though it is thought by some that it was more likely to have been a corn-grinding mill.

North of the village today there are still remnants of the Forest of Needwood, it was a hunting ground or chase reserved solely for noblemen, at one time covering 70 to 80,000 acres. The forest was divided into wards:- Tutbury, Marchington, Yoxall and Barton. It was under the rule of officers who lived within the borders of the forest, at houses called lodges:- Byrkley lodge, Yoxall lodge, Ealand lodge at Marchington and Sherholt lodge in the Barton ward.

The trees of the forest included holly, hawthorn, oak, lime, sycamore, elm, maple, wych-elm and ash. The forest animals included wild boar, horned cattle, red deer and horses. It was once written that there was a time when a squirrel could leap from tree to tree the whole length of Staffordshire, from Kinver Forest in the south of Cannock Chase, to the Needwood Forest, and on to the Peak without once setting foot on soil. The forest stretched to Sherwood in Nottinghamshire.

There were 32 gates into the forest, two of which were in Barton, the first at Barton Gate, which has retained its name to the present day. It was situated near the "Top Bell" inn. The second was Blakenhall Gate, situated on Bar Lane a short distance south of the Yoxall road. There were also ten parks attached to the forest; one of which was Barton Park, south of Barton Gate; Barton Park Farm still bears the name today. The park was in existence by 1297.

The first substantial Barton church was built in 1157 in the vicinity of the earlier Saxon church, and was dedicated to St. Mary Magdalene: it was made of timber and stone. There was a medieval tithe barn in the churchyard. The church was a chapel-of-ease to the parish of Tatenhill, of which Barton was a part. An early reference to the church in Barton is in an episcopal visitation roll of 1305. It is not certain whether this church stood on the same site as the present one, but it is thought to have been near a piece of land known as "Hall Orchard". A map of 1839 shows a field bearing this name, situated between the present church and the brook; today Church Lane housing development stands on the land. A chest from that medieval church, dated from between 1100 and 1300, is all that remains. The chest can be seen in church today.

At the time of the Domesday Book in 1086 the owner of the manor of Barton, was the king, William the Conqueror. There were other manors that today are a part of Barton parish, and some farms bear their names, for example:- Newbold Manor Farm was part of the old manor of Newbold, and Blakenhall lodge was part of Blakenhall manor.

EARLY HISTORY 13TH CENTURY TO THE 17TH CENTURY

Blakenhall Lodge was the seat of the ancient family of Minors, the first recorded being Roger de Mynors in the reign of King John. The lands and buildings left today are the modern remains of Blakenhall manor. William the Conqueror granted the manor of Barton to Henry de Ferrers and family.

The manor came into the hands of the Somerville family but at the beginning of Henry III's reign, William de Ferrers, who was the Earl of Derby gave Dunstall and Newbold manors to Walter de Somerville in exchange for Barton. It was later forfeited to the Crown again in 1263 after the rebellious conduct of Robert de Ferrers, in the Barons War (1263 to 1266). The king then created the earldom, (later to be the Duchy of Lancaster) and gave the land to his son Edmund, nicknamed "Crouchback", the first Earl of Lancaster. Tutbury Castle became the midland headquarters of the Dukes of Lancaster, and Barton was in the "honour" of Tutbury Castle, which meant it was part of a collection of manors under one lord paramount, ie. the Earl of Lancaster. It is in connection with Thomas, 2nd Earl of Lancaster, the son and successor of Edmund Crouchback, that we first meet with Richard de Holland. In 1313 he held an official position in the earl's territory of the Peak, a region then also included in the honour of Tutbury Castle. Richard was a stock- or studkeeper for the Earl of Lancaster. In 1314 he was granted "heyboot", "houseboot" and "fireboot" in the Forest of Needwood. That meant he could take wood for fence, house-repair and fuel. Richard fought with the Earl of Lancaster against king Edward II, at the battle of Burton Bridge 1322.

From 1086 to 1327 the population of Barton increased threefold. At Barton the rental of 1327 describes a quarter of the tenants of Barton itself as "bondsmen".

Early History

On the death of a virgater or bondsman, the lord of the manor had the right to take the best beast and all brass pots, iron-bound carts and wagons, beehives, uncut woollen clothes, affers and male foals, male and female pigs, whole bacons and any money if there was any.

In the 14th and 15th centuries fairs, markets, religious plays, dancing and travelling musicians were popular. Barton had "the Barton Wakes" the first Sunday in August (a type of fun fair); there were also two cattle fairs, held annually on 3rd May and 28th November. These had ceased by 1880.

Some time after 1485, King Henry VII, was hunting in Needwood Forest and became separated from his party. He met the father of John Taylor, who was to become a famous and influential person, and who had the present church built and completed by 1533. The parish register dates from 1571. Religious changes during the reign of Elizabeth I caused the church to change its name to St. James. It is suggested that this was because his was the nearest saints day on the calendar to that of Mary Magdalene. Barton's church was one of the few to escape destruction during the civil wars in 1645-51, although the church did suffer some damage; some extravagantly decorated brasses in the churchyard, dating from 1533, were removed from their stone bases. These bases can still be found in the church today. Some statues and figures in the church may also have been damaged.

Another Barton benefactor, believed to have been born in Barton in 1529, is Thomas Russell, an apprentice with the Drapers Company of London, who later became a wealthy merchant in the City of London and left money in his will for a school to be built in Barton. The building was started in 1593, completed in 1595, and was known as Russell's Free Endowed School.

Apart from the usual occupations of villagers at around this time, a lot of people of Barton were engaged in forestry work, whilst others dug marl from pits, for use in road building and as a top dressing on the fields. The soil had some unusual qualities. In 1686 when Robert Plot documented his history of Staffordshire, he wrote "Newbold manor, one mile east of Barton is occupied by a farm, and near it are several saline springs which have such an effect on the pastures, as to change the colours of the cattle that graze on them, from a black, red or brown, to a whitish dun".

The people of Barton paid tithes, the small tithes to the vicar at Barton, and the main, much greater tithe entitlement going to the rector at Tatenhill. An example of the contents of the tithe custom for 1587 reads:

> *"for the tithe of pears and apples the owner is to yield the tenth part by estimation, and the same to be fetched at his house, for cherries, plums and nuts the parson is to have a tithe, if he shall come, or send to get him a dish of the same, otherwise not".*

Under the Needwood Tree

The tithe barn stood facing the main, west door of the church and was still there in the early 20th century (the west door faces towards Collinson Road and Wales Lane).

Barton had become a Crown possession once more back in 1399, when Henry Bolingbroke became King Henry IV of England. The manor of Barton was sold by King Charles I to the city of London in 1629, large sums of money being needed by the King to carry on the heavy expense of the Civil War. Later, the manor passed into private hands, being purchased by Sir Edward Bromfield, whose son, John Bromfield, succeeded him as lord of the Manor in 1660. In 1733 the manor passed through marriage to William Busby, and later in the century to Eusebius Horton of Catton: later still the lord of the manor was Lady Wilmot Horton.

There were a number of Charities in Barton. In 1651 William Key of Sherholt Lodge, bequeathed land in Barton, to be leased or rented and the income put to charity use for the poor. Other early benefactors included William Holland, who in 1639, gave by will land for the use of the poor of Barton. The trustees were the overseers of the poor and some years later the workhouse was built on this land, with a row of almshouses added later still. In 1656 Edmund Godfrey left land for the same purpose to the same trustees, as did Sir Walter Walker when he left land rents. In 1691 Joseph Sanders, of an old Barton family, whose house was on Dunstall Road, called "Yewtrees" and later "Nuttall", left £52 for the purchase of bread for the poor. Henry Lees gave by will £5, to be paid in groats to poor widows to purchase plums for the wakes.

Barton did not have an actual manor house, certainly not after William the Conqueror's time, but the village had its manor court. Whilst under Duchy of Lancaster ownership, the Duchy appointed a steward to act as lord of the manor, generally an official from Tutbury Castle. Even when Barton was sold to the city of London, a steward was still appointed. When Barton became privately owned in the 17th century, the owners became the Lord of the Manor. The Lord of the Manor today is a Mr. D. W. H. Neilson, still of Catton Hall, Walton, and all the documents covering the manor from the 16th and 17th centuries are deposited in Derby public library with the Catton papers.

In 1662 Parliament had devised a tax known as the "Hearth Tax" quite simply a tax on fireplaces. In 1682 when Barton was visited and a complete list made for taxation purposes, there were 126 hearths, which would have realised £12 and 12 shillings. This helps to give a picture of the size of the village as we near the end of the 17th century.

Early History

There is an ancient ballad about Barton and the area that dates back many years, some consider it probably dates from the Middle Ages. The written record of it in its older form can be found as well as the turn of the century version, where it is slightly different.

The old version:
Barton's under Needwood
Dunstall's in the dale
Tatenhill's for a pretty girl
and Burton's for good ale

more recent:
The merry Bell of Barton
and Dunstall in the dale
the pretty girls of Tatenhill
and Burton famed for ale

BARTON AND THE NEEDWOOD FOREST 1682

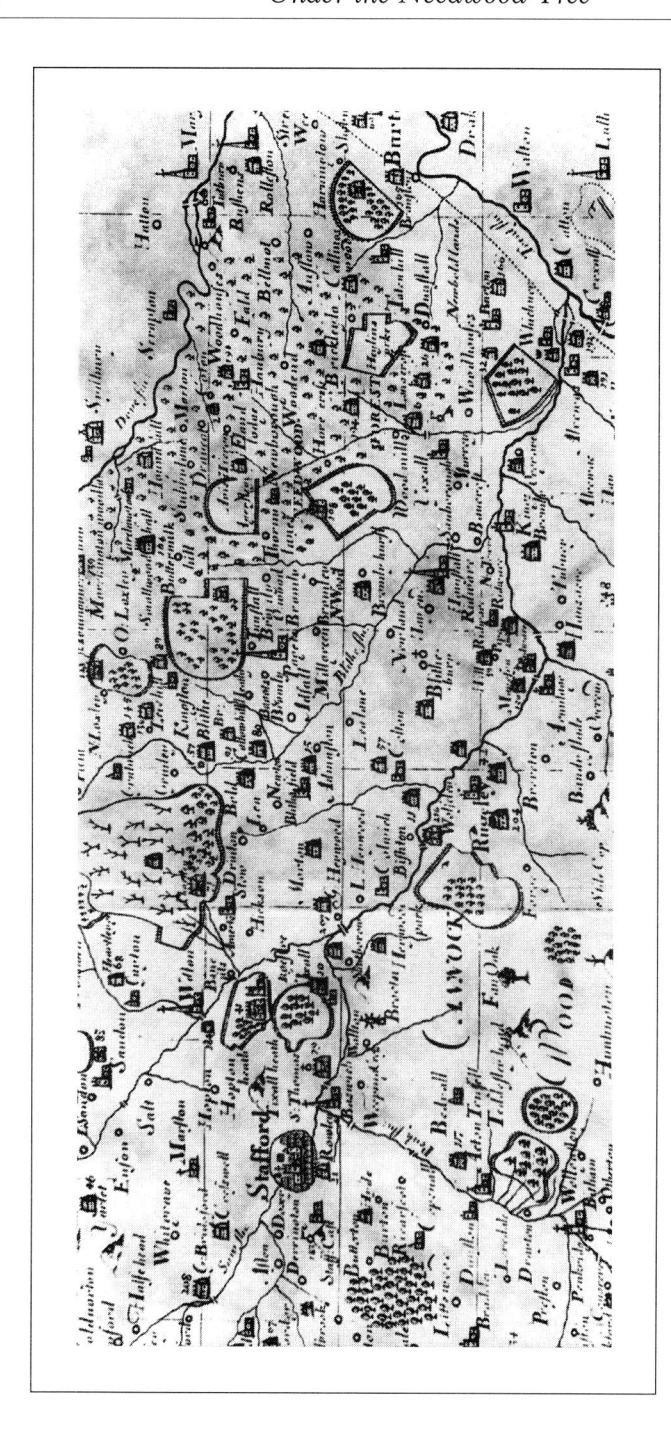

A Staffordshire map of 1682 by Robert Plot

The map shows Barton and Needwood Forest.
Plot described the map as central Staffordshire, showing Stafford, Burton and part of Cannock Chase

Chapter Two

Four Notable Ancestors from Early History

Richard De Holland

The Holland family who lived in Barton for 600 years, 1330 to 1930, descended from a Richard de Holland, or de Holand as the name was then spelt. Richard settled in Barton in the early part of the reign of Edward II. He came from Upholland in Lancashire, where a family of note had been in existence for some time. At the time of Richard de Holland both Barton and Upholland were part of the Earldom (later the Duchy) of Lancaster. Tutbury Castle, was the midland headquarters of the Earls (later Dukes) of Lancaster. Both Barton and the forest of Needwood were under control of Tutbury Castle. In 1314 the Earl of Lancaster granted Richard de Holland extensive rights and privileges in the forest of Needwood. The charter authorising these rights and privileges is printed in Shaw's *History and Antiquities of Staffordshire*, the charter reads;

> *Thomas Earl of Lancaster and Leicester, high steward of England, to whom all these present shall come, greeting; know ye that we have given, & confirmed, to Richard de Holland of Barton, and his heirs, Houseboot, Heyboot and Fireboot, and common of pasture, in our Forest of Needwood, for all his beasts, as well in places fenced as lying open, with 40 hogs, quit of pawnage in our said forest at all times in the year, except; hogs only in the fence month. All which premises we will warrant, & C. To the said Richard and his heirs against all people for ever*
> *Test. Sir Ralph de Rolleston, & confirmed given at our manor of Rockley, Dec.29. 7 EDII.*

This is a 17th century abstract of Richard's charter made by the Parliamentary Commissioners in 1650, following the execution of King Charles I, when they visited the neighbourhood with a view to sale of the forest. Richard's charter was then in the possession of Thomas Bott of Dunstall, since which time all trace of it has been lost. The terms "houseboot, heyboot and fireboot" meant that Richard and his heirs could take wood from the royal forest for repairing house, fences and for fuel. "Quit of pawnage" meant Richard and those after him were to be exempt from this customary return or payment made to the lord of the manor for permission to feed swine in the forest.

From a record to be found among the minister's accounts of the Duchy of Lancaster, dated a year earlier than the charter, 1313 we learn that Richard held an official position in the Earl's territory of the Peak, a region also in the honour of Tutbury. This record is evidence that by 1313 Richard was settled in Barton, for it was the Reeve of Barton, when submitting the Barton manorial accounts at Tutbury, who notified that 9 shillings and 10 pence had been delivered to Richard de Holland "Instaurius" of the Peak. As to what this office actually was, a leading expert on antiquarian matters at the turn of the century supplied the following information. The word "Instaurius" may be translated as stock-keeper or stud-keeper. He was the man responsible for the cattle and horses on the estate. Richard's position was one of much importance. His master was the Earl of Lancaster, and the Peak lands estate would have been large and extensive.

Unfortunately no direct proof of Richard's date of birth or origin can be found, but experts are agreed that he is one of the Hollands from Lancashire. *The Victoria County History of Lancashire* says of the family: "the Hollands were a numerous clan in south west Lancashire; their importance greatly increased with the rise of their chief". This passage then refers to Sir Robert de Holland, the head of the clan, and the position he held with the Earl of Lancaster. He was the Earl's personal secretary, and enjoyed his confidence and favour to a special degree. Among the many gifts of territory Sir Robert received from the Earl was the Manor of Yoxall, three miles from Barton, so here we have two prominent Hollands in the area at the same time. Although we do not know their actual relationship it is apparent they came from the same family.

In 1322 the Earl organised a second rebellion against King Edward II. In this rebellion, with its fatal ending for the Earl at Boroughbridge in Yorkshire, both Richard de Holland of Barton, and Sir Robert, took part. The rival armies first encountered each other at Burton-on-Trent, in 1322; the Battle of Burton Bridge, when Richard, with other supporters, including his contemporary Sir Robert, strove to prevent the royal army crossing the River Trent. Richard and his confederates broke down the bridges at Wychnor and Ridware, in a further attempt to impede the passage of the King. The Earl of Lancaster had been at Pontefract awaiting reinforcements from the King of Scotland (Robert the Bruce), but had to leave early to try to intercept the King's passage northwards, and had arrived at Tutbury Castle in the beginning of March 1322. Within days, he and 30,000 men, arrived at Burton.

Four Notable Ancestors from Early History

The following account of the battle is taken from an old chronicle of a monk of Malmesbury, being probably the oldest and therefore the most authentic account of the battle that exists:

> *The King led his army from Coventry to a large river called Trent. There is over it a large bridge which affords a passage to travellers. The King sent forward to the bridge-head a strong wedge of men-at-arms and foot soldiers, wishing to know if anyone was blocking his passage. But the Earl of Lancaster with all his retinue had entered the town of Burghtone (Burton) from the side. When it was discovered that the King purposed to cross the river, the Earl sent a brave company of armed men and foot soldiers to defend the bridge. For three or four days they skirmished, and on each morrow returned to the same sort of warfare. The King found a ford higher upstream (Walton) where he and the rest of the army crossed. The Barons hearing and actually seeing that the King had crossed the river, abandoned the bridge, mounted and fled. Why fled the Earl of Lancaster who so often stood up against the King, the more so as he had with him the Earl of Hereford, and the picked soldiery of all England? In truth the King's hand was heavy and powerful for he had all told 300,000 men. The King pursued the fugitives to Tutbury Castle, held by Lancaster; and found the gates open, because after the flight of the Earl, no one dared to resist.*

So the Earl had fled, there being no other course open to him. The only hope lay in returning as speedily as possible to Pontefract, in reach of his northern ally, the King of Scotland. So he made a hasty retreat from Tutbury across the River Dove, into Derbyshire. The River Dove was swollen by heavy rains, and in crossing at a ford, the Earl lost a large part of his treasure.

The treasure was lost in the river and lay hidden for over five centuries, until it was discovered accidentally in June 1831, by cotton mill workmen, employed by the Burton mill owners to develop the embankments of the river. This find started a mini gold rush, but after a week the Crown asserted its rights to the treasure. In all it was estimated that 100,000 coins were recovered. Many of these coins are now in the British Museum.

The Earl was overtaken at Boroughbridge. In the bloody battle that followed he was totally defeated, taken prisoner and beheaded at Pontefract. Sir Robert de Holland surrendered to the King at Derby and escaped penalty of death though he languished for a while in various prisons. Eventually he was set free upon giving a pledge of good behaviour. Richard de Holland had to face the courts for his part in damage to the bridges, and these circumstances are recorded in the following plea rolls for the County of Stafford:

> *The jury of the hundred of Pirhull presented that Richard de Holland, William Malveysin, Ralph le Walker, Richard de Stretton and Gilbert Henri, during Lent in 15 E 11(1322), were at the bridge at Burton assisting the Earl of Lancaster against the King, and that the*

said Richard de Holland of Barton, and Gilbert Henri, at the time the King was pursueing the said Earl and his rebels, broke down the bridges at Rydware and Whichnor, to impede the passage of the King. The Sherriff was therefore ordered to attach them, and the said William Malveysin, Gilbert Henri and Richard de Holland of Barton afterwards appeared, and being questioned respecting the premises stated they were not guilty, and put themselves on the country, and the jury said that Richard de Holland and William Malveysin were guilty, and they were committed to the custody of the marshal. Richard and William later appeared and could not deny the above transgression, they were committed again to the custody of the marshal. William Malveysin afterwards made fine with the King for 20 shillings and found surety. Richard de Holland made fine for 40 shillings by the surety of Thomas de Rolleston, Richard de Calangwode, John le Rouse, Robert de Barton, clerk etc who stood for bail for his good behaviour in future.

Richard de Holland's name appears many times over the years in records, as a witness to deeds and important matters in Barton, the last mention found was in 1343, where he witnessed a deed.

Richard de Holland and Richard his son were two of several witnesses to a charter of property in Dunstall made by Sir Philip de Sommerville, KNT, Lord of Wychnor to Hugh de Newbold, dated at Wychnor, Thursday next after the feast of St. Martin, the 16th of ED.III ad 1343

In 1387, 40 years after the above deed, the jury in a view of frankpledge found that Richard de Holland of Barton was feloniously murdered at night on the feast of St. John, by his wife Joan and Thomas Graunger, an armourer. This case was a famous one of its day, and many years later in (1414), when Henry V came to Lichfield to examine the state of lawlessness in Staffordshire, the case was heard again. The disordered state existed, due to unsettled conditions arising from constant wars at home and abroad. The number of assaults, robberies, murders and burnings committed by all types of people was incredible.

The main information on the Hollands of Barton from Richard II, until Tudor times, is gathered from court rolls; they recorded all the proceedings that took place at the manor and forest courts, later to be called "woodmotes". In these court rolls the Hollands are named continuously as jurors, and those who fixed the fines imposed in court; and they appear, too, as offenders from time to time. Richard de Holland is mentioned in a woodmote court roll for 1336, that he was fined 6 pence for taking away a cartload of old undergrowth. At another woodmote a similar sum was imposed on a William Atte Wode for cutting of old undergrowth at the gate of Richard de Holland. William Atte Wode was the Reeve of Barton.

Four Notable Ancestors from Early History

In 1538, long after Richard de Holland, Henry VIII ordered a muster of his entire armed force throughout the country. The army was never actually called up, but among the muster rolls taken at Barton-under-Needwood were the following:

Richard Holland (a descendant of Richard de Holland) Horse harnes, Bill able.
Richard Holland the younger, Gesturne, Salet, Splentes, Bill without horse.
William Holland Billman without horse or Harnes.
Nicholas Holland Billman without horse or Harnes.

"Harnes" was a term used to describe all types of defensive armour. A "bill" was a pike with a long handle and spearhead with a billhook, often 18 feet in length and used to pull a man off his horse.

A "gesturne" was a jacket without sleeves, with overlapping oblong plates of steel.

A "salet" was a light steel cap, extending over the nape of the neck. "Splentes" was armour for the arms, worn with a gesturne.

In 1639 a William Holland died and left his land by will for use of the poor. In 1682 when Barton was visited for the purpose of assessing the 'Hearth Tax' there were several Hollands on the list chargeable for their hearths. There was a Mrs. Holland, a widow, a Richard, a William, and again a William Holland. One of these William Hollands was made trustee of "Key's charity" (see William Key). There were many Hollands over the next few hundred years on the Barton side of this honourable family. Many had distinguished careers in the Church and the Army: Herbert St. Barbe Holland became Archdeacon of Warwick, Rev. William Holland and Dr. Tristam Holland worked for many years with the medical mission in India. Many Hollands are buried in Barton churchyard, having lived in the family patrimonial estate, and old family house known as "Holland House", which stood on Station Road, but today is the site of Meadow Rise housing development.

The other side of the family, the Hollands of Lancashire, is a fascinating story, the remarkable careers of the ennobled Hollands stand out as striking and romantic in English history, playing an active part in its most chivalrous period. They won the highest honours for services rendered and became allied by marriage with the highest in the land, being amongst the first Knights of the Order of the Garter. Their branch of the stem at remote Upholland in Lancashire enjoyed favourable conditions, shot rapidly forth, grew to a great height, and flourished a while, then broke off and died at the closing period of the Middle Ages.

In 1929 a book was published entitled *Some records of the Holland family*. It was a life's research by William Richard Holland, of Holland House, Barton. William had died before he could publish the book, but his daughter, Miss Mary Holland, the last of the family to live in Barton (until the 1950s), had the book published in his memory. Holland House and the Holland family are gone from Barton but the name still lives on, in Holland Park, a housing development opposite where Holland House stood, and the Holland Sports Club, which stands on land donated by the Holland family.

JOHN TAYLOR (died 1534, probable date of birth 1480)

At some time around 1480 triplet sons were born to Joan, wife of William Taylor, who was probably employed as a game warden in the forest of Needwood, although some historians suspect he may have been a tailor. It was unusual, 500 years ago, for triplets to be born, and to be healthy and live to adulthood was extraordinary. The family, John the first born, his brothers Rowland and Nathaniel and their sister Elizabeth lived in a cottage, probably in the area north east of the church, where several of the village's oldest timberframed cottages still stand today. Some suspect that a cottage on Main Street, directly opposite the church, and adjoining an estate agent's premises, may be the site of the Taylor's cottage. To date no evidence has come to light to pinpoint the exact spot. Members of the Taylor family had lived in Barton since 1345, and William and Joan took possession of their cottage in 1471.

The story of the triplets' life has a folk-tale quality about it. Robert Plot, writing his history of Staffordshire in 1686, tells of triplet babies being presented to King Henry VII as a rarity. The King was so impressed that he undertook to pay for their education. But this story seems to be somewhat romanticised. The descendants of the family give 1480 as the year of the triplets' birth. Yet we know that Henry VII did not accede to the throne until 1485, so it is unlikely that he was shown newborn babes; it is far more probable that they were growing lads.

So the story probably goes, as legend suggests, that the King was on a hunting foray in the Forest of Needwood (it is known that members of the royal families frequently came to Tutbury Castle), the King became detached from his party and was lost. It was late and dark when the wandering King came across William Taylor, either in the forest or by arriving at his cottage. The King was introduced to William's wife and was shown the three healthy boys. It is known that the King was very impressed, and may well have seen the three as a symbol of the Holy Trinity. William Taylor escorted the King to Tutbury Castle, and the King was most grateful, and pledged he would pay for the triplets to be educated if they grew to manhood. They did and the King was true to his word. From this event the royal bounty for triplets was instigated and only ceased during the present reign.

Four Notable Ancestors from Early History

All three of the Taylor boys are said to have entered the learned professions after being educated at university "beyond the seas", probably in France or Italy. There is a note in the royal privy purse expenses of 1498 which reads:

for the wages of the Kings scoler, John Taillor at Oxenford.

John Taylor obtained the degrees of Doctor of Civil Law and Doctor of Canon Law. By virtue of those degrees he was incorporated in Cambridge University in 1520 and Oxford two years later. Long before John Taylor received his academic honours from the English universities he had received much preferment in church and state. In 1503 John Taylor was ordained and held his first living as Rector at Bishop's Hatfield. In 1504 he was sent to negotiate a commercial treaty with Philip of Burgundy. He was in fact a Tudor civil servant. The following year he became Rector of Sutton Coldfield. By 1509 he had become Prebendary of Eccleshall in Lichfield diocese, and was one of the royal chaplains at Henry VII's funeral.

John Taylor was a pluralist clergyman, taking the incomes from seven or eight churches, and paying another to take services. Here is a summary of most of the positions he held and their incomes. They were all held at different times and for different durations.

Post	£	s.	d.
Vicar—Bishop's Hatfield	33	2	1
Vicar—Sutton Coldfield	33	9	2
Vicar—Eccleshall	20	0	0
Vicar—All Hallows the Great	41	18	1
Vicar—Coldingham	10	0	0
Archdeacon—Derby	26	12	4
Archdeacon—Buckingham	87	14	7
Vicar—St. Gabriel, Fenchurch Street	12	0	0
Canon—St. Stephen's, Westminster	30	0	0
Vicar—Halifax	84	13	6
Vicar—Skyrby	33	0	0
Clerk to Parliament	40	0	0
Master of the Rolls	34	0	0
Livery	7	5	4
Robes	3	11	0
Allowance for a journey to Rome (trip did not actually take place)	266	13	4

Annual remuneration is shown in the table above (£ s. d.).

Under the Needwood Tree

The new King Henry VIII appointed John Taylor as King's Clerk and Chaplain, and two years later he was made Clerk to the Parliament, Master in Chancery, the Receiver of Petitions, Vicar of All Hallows in London and Rector of Coldingham. John Taylor was fast becoming a rich and influential man. In June 1513 he accompanied Henry VIII on a campaign in France. For four months he kept a detailed diary which has proved most valuable to historians. John Taylor was an eye-witness of Henry's victories at Theroane, Lille and Tournay. He records the terrible storms, rain and mud that the army had to endure, and how their tents were blown down. The diary can be seen today in the British Museum. John was entrusted with delicate tasks. He wrote the King's Speech for the Dissolution of Parliament in 1514, and acted as host to the Venetian Ambassador in 1515.

In 1515 John Taylor became Archdeacon of Derby, in 1516 Archdeacon of Buckingham, Prebendary of St. Stephen's at Westminster and Prolocutor of Convocation. He gave the official replies to the Spanish envoys, and by 1517 he was deputising for the Master of the Rolls.

John Taylor decided to build a new church in the village of his birth, never having forgotten the place and circumstances of his early years. He obtained permission from the King to erect a chapel, which replaced the 1157 Chapel of Ease to Tatenhill. Barton was in the Parish of Tatenhill. No trace of the earlier church remains except the oak parish chest. It was said that John Taylor's church was built on or near the site of his parents' cottage. The year that work was started is recorded as 1517, it is carved on the south side of the tower. Inside the church, inscriptions over alternate pillars of the nave tell of John Taylor's career, together with representations of his coat of arms, the head and shoulders of three children and a Tudor rose.

John became Royal Ambassador to Burgundy and France and was present at the famous meeting of Henry VIII and Francis I of France, called "The Field of the Cloth of Gold". The meeting was in June 1520, in northern France. It was intended to strengthen peace ties between the two nations and was masterminded by the great Cardinal Wolsey. Each King and court strove to outshine the other. Henry was accompanied by 5,000 people, and spent £13,000 on the splendour of the occasion, a vast amount of money at that time. John Taylor was one of the ten chaplains who accompanied the King. The English built a splendid pavilion, a temporary palace of wood and canvas, with window upon window created by the Flemish glazier, Galyon Hone. Fine malmsey and claret flowed from drinking fountains. The elaborate name of the meeting came from the extravagant tents that the French erected and the amazing display of wealth by both Kings. Finally no agreement could be reached.

In 1527 John Taylor was made Master of the Rolls. In the same year he was sent to France, to invest Francis I with the Order of the Garter. John Taylor was later appointed as one of the commissioners to try the validity of Henry VIII's marriage to Catherine of Aragon. In 1528 he became the Archdeacon of Halifax and 1529 saw him take his seat in the first Reformation Parliament.

By 1533, after a two-year stay in France as English Ambassador, John Taylor was generally considered to be next in line for a bishopric, when one should become vacant. It seems possible that Wolsey had been using John Taylor in vain to try to find a suitable French Princess to be future Queen of England, should Henry's divorce be granted. Wolsey's dread of Anne Boleyn was well known. By now ill-health was affecting John Taylor, he was suffering with a diseased leg. Suddenly pressure was on him to surrender his prebend at St. Stephen's, Westminster; whether it was due to ill-health or, that he fell out of royal favour, we do not know. In 1534 John Taylor wrote his will and resigned as Master of the Rolls in favour of Thomas Cromwell.

John Taylor died before the end of 1534, but at least he had seen his church completed in 1533. It seems strange that the place of his burial has not been traced, though it is thought there was a monument to him erected in St. Anthony's Church in Threadneedle Street, London. Some historians think it possible that John Taylor was killed after he fell from royal favour, but no evidence supporting this has ever been found, except that his grave cannot be traced; and some believe that his will may well have been a forgery, or certainly part of it, as John spells his name in at least three different ways, Taylor, Tailer and Taylour, which suggests that he did not write all of it. This type of practice was not uncommon at this time in history.

John Taylor left various bequests to churches at Shetesbrook in Berkshire, Bishops Hatfield and Lincoln Cathedral. His servants, sister Elizabeth and executors, nephews and cousins shared the contents of his considerable household at Bethnal Green, and there were many other bequests. There are descendants of John and of Rowland Taylor alive today, although very little is known of John's wife and children, mainly because clergy were not officially supposed to marry, though it seems many did. Celibacy of the clergy in the Church of England was not abolished until 1549. A family named "Garnet-Taylor" were descendants of the family; they lived at "Yew Tree House" next to the Shoulder of Mutton Inn in the mid to late 19th century. It is believed that the only relative alive today of John Taylor is a Mrs Christie in Australia.

A touching sentence that John Taylor wrote in Latin before he died reads:

> *Nothing in the world is more fleeting than human life, nothing follows more certainly than death, nothing is more uncertain than the hour of our death, and how transitory are the worldly goods provided for us by the goodness of God.*

The High School in Barton under Needwood bears John Taylor's name to record local pride in his illustrious career. The knowledge that he rose from lowliness to eminence through education and application to duty is an example to today's young people, and his church assures that he will never be forgotten in Barton-under-Needwood.

THOMAS RUSSELL (1529-1593)

Thomas Russell is clearly one of the most remarkable sons of Barton-under-Needwood, for his achievements were due to his own initiative and not as a result of patronage. By sheer hard work and business acumen he became a wealthy and powerful Merchant Draper in the City of London in the latter part of the sixteenth century, owning a 'Greate Warehouse' and a shop, together with a great deal more property in the City and the surrounding area. The site of some of his property now lies beneath London's Liverpool Street Railway Station.

Although there is no proof of his date of birth, for the Barton Church Register did not start until 1571 and there are no contemporary written records, we can assume that he was born in 1529. The first definite mention of Thomas Russell is in a ledger entry at Drapers' Hall in London, dated 1543, which records him being bound as an apprentice draper. Since the usual age of starting an apprenticeship was fourteen, we can place his year of birth with some confidence.

How, then do we know that Thomas came from Barton-under-Needwood? Well, the evidence, although circumstantial, is nevertheless overwhelming.

One of Thomas's sisters, Joane, married Thomas Bailey, a yeoman farmer, and they lived at Handsacre, near Armitage. His niece, Margery, married Thomas Temple of Barton and they were married in St. James's Church in 1573. Thomas owned land in Barton and Dunstall and, when he died, some of this land was left to John Holland of Barton, and the rest was sold by his executors. He left money to the churches at Barton, Colton and Blithfield for the purchase and distribution of bread for the poor, and all three churches have charity boards recording the details.

But, above all, we remember Thomas Russell for providing sufficient money in his Will for the building and maintenance of a school in Barton, and for further providing the necessary funds to pay for the salaries of the Master and the Usher.

The money for the construction of the school was entrusted to the Rev. Adrian Saravia, the Rector of Tatenhill Parish, (which then included Barton), and it was he who was responsible for the school being built between Thomas Russell's death, in 1593, and 1595, when the school opened. The records of the Duchy of Lancaster show that several loads of timber were brought to Barton from Needwood Forest during the school's construction.

Four Notable Ancestors from Early History

The school was administered by the Drapers' Company, in accordance with Thomas Russell's wishes, until shortly after the 1870 Education Act. In the history of the Drapers' Company this was very important, for Barton School was the first of many educational establishments to be administered by the Company. Local dignitaries were appointed as 'visitors' and they kept the Drapers' Company informed about the school's progress.

The following passage, taken from a letter written from the Barton 'visitors' to the Drapers' Company in London in the year 1600, makes it quite clear that the people of Barton regarded Thomas as a local man. It reads:

> *Whereas Master Thomas Russell, one of your companye latelie deceased, hath a greate charitie towards his native countrey to his singular commendacon erected a schoole heare at Barton in Staffordshire and given continuall mayntenance for a Schoole Master and Usher...*

Of the Rector of Tatenhill, Adrian Saravia, there is insufficient space here to do justice to his colourful and exciting career; suffice it to say that he was a theologian, born in the Spanish Netherlands. He became a Professor of Theology at Leiden University and, later, its Chancellor. He was well known to Lord Burghley, Sir Francis Walsingham and the Earl of Leicester. In 1588 he had to make a sudden departure from the Netherlands, due partly to religious and military turmoils, but also to political intrigue. He arrived in London and Queen Elizabeth, wishing to give him protection, presented him with the living at Tatenhill. He remained there from 1588 to 1595, during which time he was involved with Thomas Russell's school. As Thomas had mentioned Saravia by name in his Will, it would be interesting to know whether the two men had ever met, for the Dutch Church in London is only a short distance from Drapers' Hall.

The Rev. Saravia left Tatenhill in 1595 in order to take up the post of Canon of Canterbury Cathedral. He was well known for several theological treatises he had written in the latter part of his life and, when King James I came to the throne, he was asked to join a group of scholars in translating parts of the Bible for the Authorised Version.

Thomas Russell's school became known as Barton Free School and, if it was built according to his instructions, it would have housed seventy pupils. He wanted it to be a copy of the recently built (1573) Barnet Grammar School in Middlesex of which he himself was a Founder Governor. Unless a picture of the school comes to light we shall never know what it looked like, for it was demolished prior to 1885 and replaced by the present building. However, we do know its size, because the 1883 Ordnance Survey map shows the ground plan.

Thomas Russell died on the 23rd July, 1593 and, if his declared wish was carried out, he was buried at the church of St. Edmund the King in Lombard Street in the City of London.

In his lifetime he showed generosity and compassion to those less fortunate than himself. He displayed great loyalty to his friends, relations, employees and, especially, to his place of birth. In providing Barton-under-Needwood with a school, he showed a forward-looking concern for the education and welfare of future generations. If Thomas could see the schools we have in Barton today, he would be well pleased, and this would provide him with some reward for his past generosity.

The village is very fortunate to have had such a benefactor.

WILLIAM KEY

Little is known about the life of William Key, a 17th century land owner, who lived at Sherholt Lodge and bequeathed some land in 1651 to be leased or rented and the income put to charitable use for the good of the poor of Barton-under-Needwood and Dunstall. One of the conditions of the charity, which is still carried out today, is that the vicar must preach a sermon on Good Friday and be paid the sum of ten shillings (50 pence) for doing so.

The following entries are in the Parish Register: "12th June 1650 Margarett, wife of William Key buried" and "11th October 1651 Gulielmus Key, de Sherhold Logd buried". Gulielmus is the Latin form of William. In the church is a brass tablet to the memory of William Key, gent. keeper of Barton ward, who died October 10th 1651, aged 69, and gave several charities to this town etc. and forty pounds, to buy lands with, for the poor of Tutbury. There is a gap in the records of the Parish Register around the time of the birth of William, around 1583. A number of entries mention Richard Key or Richardi Kay with respect to his children and his burial in 1617, so this may be the father of William our benefactor.

From the Charities Commissioners' reports 1839 Ex: from the 7th report of January 1822:

> *The benefaction table in St. James' Church records that William Key, late keeper of Barton ward, who died on 10th October 1651, perpetuated the annual profits of two closes, in Barton, called Lincroft and Bonthorne, and of two acres arable the one upon Collier's Flat and the other upon Spellow, to the uses following that is to say, 10s. thereof for a sermon, yearly, upon every Good Friday, to be preached within the chapel of Barton, by an orthodox minister lawfully qualified, and the residue of the whole profits to be divided into five parts; whereof one part, yearly, to be disposed for the necessary repairs of the chapel aforesaid; one other part to be annually distributed to the poor of the village of Dunstall, after*

the sermon ended; and the other three remaining parts likewise to the poor within the chapelry of Barton aforesaid, after the ministerial blessing pronounced upon the auditory.

An ancient parish book contains an entry which appears to be the substance of the will of William Key. It states that he gave by his will, one close of meadow or pasture copyhold, containing about 5 acres, more or less, adjoining to a certain common called Lincroft on the west, and Mr. Thomas Cowper's Stew, at Sandyford on the east; one other close of pasture or meadow, freehold, containing about 4 acres, more or less, lying at Bonthorne and adjoining to a close, called the Heathley's on the north abutting upon a common lane, called the Heaflinch Lane on the west, one acre of arable land, more or less, lying on Rowmeadow Furlong upon a flat there called the Spellow; one other acre of arable land, more or less, lying in the Riddings upon a flat there, called Collier's Flat, the yearly profits of which said two closes and arable land, the said William Key did give to the uses thereafter mentioned; adding that it was to be distributed by the chapelwardens at the discretion of Mr. Thomas Cowper, Mr. William Holland, and Mr. Walter Grane, and their heirs, being appointed, by the said William Key, trustees for that purpose.

The Parish is in enjoyment of the freehold close of pasture in Bonthorne which contains five acres. But it appears that only a part of the copyhold close adjoining the Lincroft Common was taken by the Parish under the will, the remaining part of the close appearing to have been since obtained in exchange for the two acres of arable land. The whole close, as it is now in possession by the Parish, contains five acres. An allotment was made out of waste lands in Lincroft Common and Brown's Lane, under the Parish enclosure containing two acres, and another out of the forest land containing one acre.

The trustees at the time of the Charities Commissioners' report of 1839, were Thomas Webb and John Holland, who had large landed estates in the area. Lincroft Close was on lease to Stephen Hawkesworth and Charles Mold, as churchwardens, and was under-let by them in many small pieces of garden ground to poor parishioners at easy rents. Bonthorne Close was let to William Rowley and the allotments in Lincroft and Brown's Lane were held by John Shilton; the forest allotment was held by Thomas Gray.

The Charities Commissioners reported that the sum of 10s was deducted for the sermon preached by the minister of Barton on Good Friday; one fifth of the remainder was retained by the churchwardens for repair of St. James' Church; one fifth was paid to officers of Dunstall to be distributed to the poor of that township; and three fifths were paid to the poor of Barton. The money was given away, on Good Friday, at the workhouse in sums varying from 3s to 10s.

Under the Needwood Tree

The beneficence of William Key is still carried out today under the auspices of the trustees for the Henry Warford and William Key Charities. The income of the William Key charity is raised by renting the land at Bonthorne, the allotments opposite Bonthorne Farm in Dogshead Lane and the adjacent field known as Bonthorne Common; and the land at Lincroft, the field adjacent to the A38 on the area known as 'Fatholme' between Barton Turns and 'Catholme'.

Under the Needwood Tree

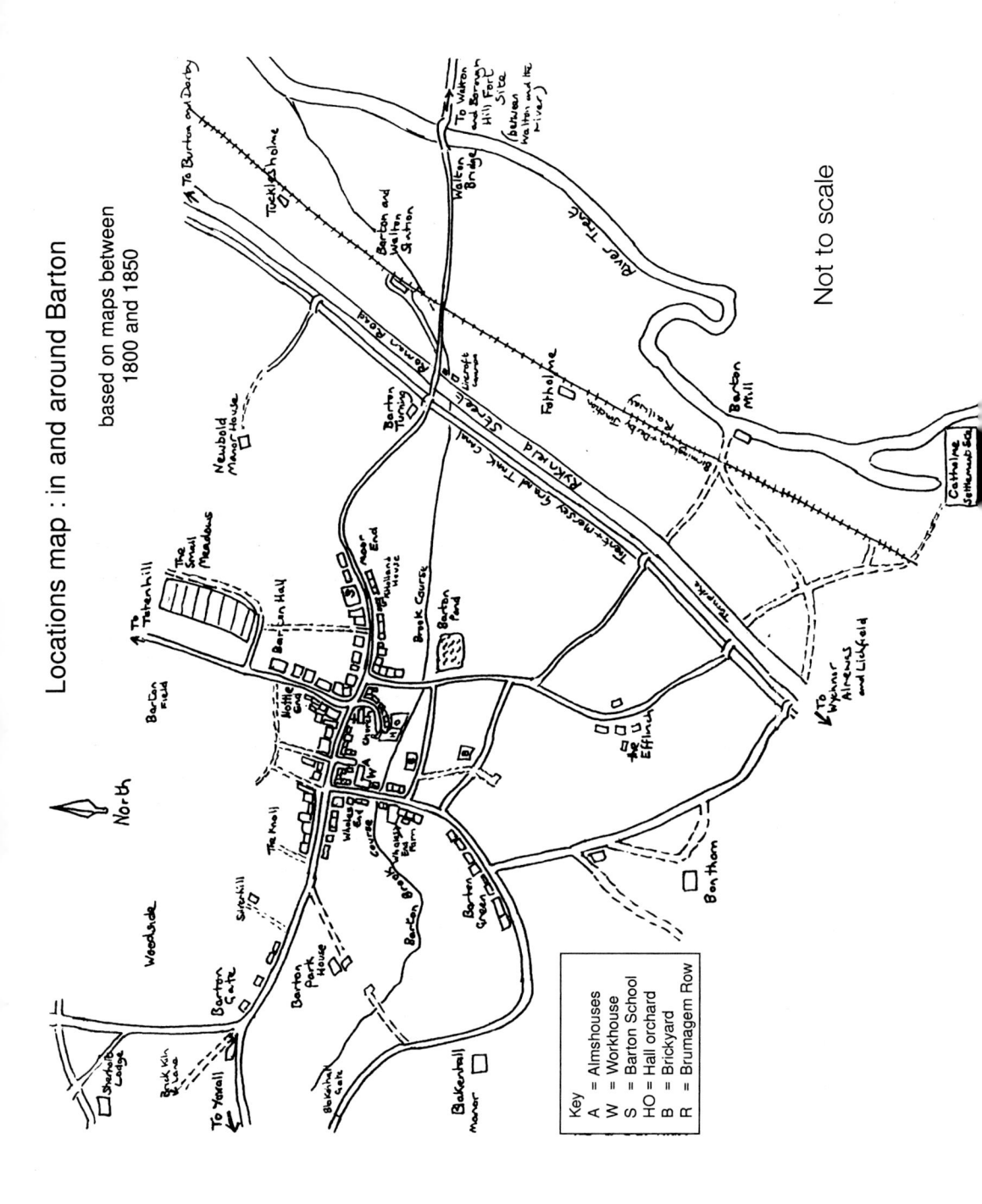

Chapter Three

BARTON IN THE 18TH AND 19TH CENTURIES

VERY little changed in the size and shape of the village for many years, but towards the second half of the 18th century came the transport revolution. It started with the building of the Trent and Mersey Grand Trunk Canal. Leading up to the canal's completion in 1777, Barton would have seen large groups of migrant workers (navvies) constructing this grand trunk canal, and linking the River Trent with the Mersey. The Act of Parliament giving permission for the canal was passed in 1776. The canal must have made quite an impact on Barton's quiet agricultural community. There are a number of hump-back canal bridges along the Barton section, and a grade 2 listed, 18th century wharf-house at Barton Turns. Indeed the name "Barton Turns", or "Turning" as it used to be, came about because the barges used to turn around, in a wide, basin-type stretch of the canal after delivering to the wharf, to return whence they came.

At the present time, the powers of parish councils are relatively few, but in the 18th century things were rather different. There were four main types of official in Barton-under-Needwood: the constable, the churchwardens, the overseers of the poor and the surveyor of highways and bridges. These officials were elected by the inhabitants, apart from the Surveyor of Highways who was elected by the local Justices of the Peace, though usually from names suggested by the community. There were usually two churchwardens, two overseers, a constable and a surveyor. They were all expected to keep records of monies collected and spent. These records had to be presented at the end of a year's term of office to the vestry, or the justice of the peace. As these official positions were unpaid the keeping of the records varied enormously. The officials were usually well off financially, and literate.

By the 18th century the constable was the executive authority in the parish and carried a staff of office to bear witness to his importance. This has not survived. The constable was usually male, (the only recorded exception in Barton is that of Alice

Holland in 1734) and served for only one year, though there were occasional exceptions. The job was onerous and varied. It was not defined by statute, as the overseer's and surveyor's duties were. The surviving annual accounts of Barton's constables are somewhat sketchy; between 1700 and 1780 they consist of merely a brief statement of income and expenditure with a balance which was often negative.

Example:

> *OCTr.ye 21/1740 (21st Oct.1740) the accompts of John Rotchford, Constable for the years 1739 to 1740 recd. of the old constable £1 5 shillings 11 pence disbursed £5 4 shillings 2 pence due from ye town to John Rotchford £3 18 shillings 1 penny allowed by us, Will. Fisher, Isaac Mousley, Philip Smith, Thomas Coates, Edward Crannidge.*

The accounts of Thomas Dilkes, Constable from October 1780 to October 1781, give an insight into his job.

Myself and horse to Lichfield and expence	*2 shillings*
gave to vagrants	*6 pence*
gave to a soldier to pass	*1 shilling*
paid Ironmonger for repair to forest gate	*1 shilling*
paid Mr. Cooper for warrants for house, land and window tax	*4 shillings*

The primary duty of the constable was to maintain watch and ward in the parish, taking in charge any committing a felony. An account in 1802 reads:

> *April 22 going to justice with Rd. Price 2 shillings April 23 putting a man in a dark hole and going to justice 2 shillings 6 pence*

The village was generally law-abiding, and because of its position, just off the main routes it rarely attracted criminals. The walk into the village probably deterred the working navvies and canal fraternity from coming to the village, especially as their needs were catered for at the thriving hamlet of Barton Turns. By 1757 the constable had the responsibility added to his tasks of providing the militia lists for the king's armies.

There are many references in the accounts to the preparation of militia lists and their delivery to Lichfield and Whittington. All these duties involved numerous journeys to Wychnor where the local J.P. resided, but journeys to the High Constable took the constable to Stafford. The constable found himself dealing with matters that were not really his responsibility, eg: paying for repairs to the workhouse, school, and the church gates, maintenance of fences for the forest markers and gates, and the pinfold (home of stray animals), the provision of coffins, and repairs to picks and wheelbarrows.

The alehouses were supposedly supervised by the constable, who was responsible for seeing that gaming and disorderly houses did not occur. Barton seems to have had few problems on this score. There is a reference in 1792 to the summoning of a brewer and the granting of a licence. There are references also to payment for ale supplied for firemen. Finally the constable had to be present at the quarterly report to the county on the state of the village.

The second oldest of the parish offices was the position of churchwarden. The wardens were elected annually at the Easter vestry meeting, one by the people and one by the vicar. The wardens' duties went far beyond the bounds of the parish church; it was, and still is, a legal position, and on appointment they had to swear an oath of loyal obedience to the bishop. The records of the wardens are similar to those of the constable. Much of the warden's work was connected with the church, its fabric and its services. In 1739 the churchwardens, Edward Crainidge and William Fisher, had their names recorded on the church bells that were cast that year and still hang today in the bell tower. There were six bells, inscribed as follows:

1. *Peace and good neighbourhood 1739. A.R. (diameter 2ft 8ins)*
2. *Prosperity to all our benefactors. 1739. A.R.(diameter 2ft 10ins)*
3. *Prosperity to the Church of England. 1739. A.R.(diameter 3ft)*
4. *We were all cast at Gloucester by Abel Rudhal 1739. A.R. (diameter 3ft 2ins)*
5. *Edward Crainidge and William Fisher, churchwardens 1739. A.R. (diameter 3ft 4ins)*
6. *I to the church the living call and to the grave do summon all 1739. A.R. (diameter 3ft 9ins)*

Two more bells were added to complete the peal before 1929, when they were all taken out and re-tuned and the belfry strengthened at a cost of over £200.

Among the most regular outgoings were bills for repairs to the churchyard wall, attention to hinges, pins and latches to the various gates, and frequent payments for the floor of the church to be "broken up" to lay to rest the bodies of faithful parishioners (people were buried in lime under the church floor). An extract from the churchwardens' accounts for 1774 reads:

"paid Mason & co for bricking Mr. Biddulph's grave, 4 shillings" and
"rec,d of Mr. Biddulph for breaking church floor, 6 shillings"

The church clock also had to be kept in good order and Mr. Rea, clockmaker of Walton, regularly came to attend the church clock. Mr. Rea's pendulum still hangs on the tower wall.

"1781 John Rea, a bill 5 shillings."

Frequent purchase of bricks, gravel, planks, oak boards, beams, wedges and metal filings bear witness to the warden's concern to keep the church and its surrounding area in good repair. In 1770 the windows underwent a major restoration, and again in 1793. Rushes for strewing the floors were provided twice a year, and lime appears in many of the bills, for lime-wash of the walls and sprinkling on the bodies under the church floor.

Each year the parish church was visited by the bishop, or his representative, when the wardens had to report on the state of the fabric and the parsonage house. There were several parsonage houses through the ages, one of which is 'the Old Parsonage' next to the churchyard on Main Street. In 1829 it was stated that the bishop found the church "a handsome Gothic stone building", generally the fabric and furnishings were in good order, but the altar cloth was in poor condition, one of the bells was cracked, and the gutters and water-spouts were in need of replacement, the floor of some pews was to be repaired, and the churchyard wall in some places was to be built up. The bishop also noted that the altar rails were to be repaired and said the Sunday school boys were to be removed from within the said rails. When the Bishop returned he found the church and its precincts "much improved since my last visit, the church neat and clean". But he ordered the Bible on the reading desk to be repaired, and the gate on the north side of the church, used for carriages at weddings, to be closed or taken away as it was unnecessary.

Not all of the churchwarden's jobs were ecclesiastical. The destruction of vermin came within their province: sparrows were recognised as a pest and payment was made on production of the heads, usually by the dozen; the bodies would find their way into a sparrow pie which was regarded as a delicacy. The wardens took the precaution of cutting the birds' heads in half, after payment was made. This payment was a major duty in Barton; long lists of payouts for huge quantities of sparrows' heads and the names of the recipients are recorded:

1774 example:

William Cranidge	3 doz	6 pence
William Holland son	2 doz	4 pence
Daniel Badkin	1 doz	2 pence
Ely Pointon	1 doz	1 penny

The churchwardens of Barton were spared the responsibility of looking after the poor, but they were required to administer and pay out the many small charities, which are recorded on the wooden boards on the walls of the priest's vestry in St. James's Church. The wardens kept the charity accounts distinct from their own general accounts. Benefactors from the 18th century included in 1728 Thomas Goodman, who gave by will £10 for use by the poor. In 1733 a Lady Bromfield and a Mrs. Bailey gave £20 each for the same. In 1750 Mr. J. Holland and William Alsop gave £20 by will for the poor, in 1758 Priscilla Allen the same and in 1778 Thomas Webb gave by will £50. In 1781 Elizabeth Busby gave £100 in her lifetime for the poor, and Martha Busby gave £20 to buy Bibles for poor children. As with the constable the general term of office for churchwardens was one year, though many would undertake the job several times at intervals throughout their lives.

The third parish official active in the 18th century was the Surveyor of the Highways and Bridges, whose office dates back to the Highways Act of 1555. The surveyor's responsibility was the maintenance of the roads and bridges within the parish boundaries. He was supposed to carry out regular inspections of these and report their condition to the quarter sessions which met at Stafford. In order to keep the roads in good repair the surveyor could call upon the able-bodied men of the parish to provide six days free labour per year. It was an unpopular office, and in the early days of the act parishes selected ineffective officials, so in the 18th century, the appointment of the surveyor was vested in the Justices of the Peace. There are very few remaining records of this particular office, but the accounts of 1783 show the surveyor was involved in the purchase of materials for road repair.

> "1783 Jany. 28
> For drawing 4 hundred of bricks from Blackenhall to make that suff at Edward Shorthoses
>   1 shilling 6 pence
> paid Thos. Cowox and John Mould for laying it   2 shillings
> paid John Mould for letting the water off the road   2 shillings
> paid Richard Badkin for getting gravil   2 shillings 10 pence"

The surveyor was responsible for supplying tools and other paid labour. As to the actual workers involved, the limited evidence suggests that paupers were employed in this task and that the overseers received money from the surveyor for this purpose.

The fourth office was the overseers of the poor, in common with the rest of England it was a system for helping those in need in Barton in the 18th century, based on the Poor Law Act of 1601. The act made every parish responsible for the care of its own poor. The cost was met by a rate on all property in the parish and the act defined the duties of the overseer and who was to receive relief.

Overseers had to be approved by two Justices of the Peace, and some could hold dual office, constable and overseer at the same time. They had to be literate to keep written accounts. The duties of the overseer were clear, and so too were the penalties; some examples are:

> *"Overseers to meet with churchwardens once a month on Sunday afternoon, to confer, consider and take order for setting to work; all children of such within parish not thought able to keep and maintain them, by all persons married and unmarried having no means to support themselves.   PENALTY:- 20 shillings fine, each".*

> *"To provide relief for such persons as are lame, old, blind, poor and unable to work within Town or Parish"*

> *"To collect tithes from every occupier of lands, houses, coal mines or saleable underwoods"*

> *"You must receive any persons removed from another parish to yours.   PENALTY:- £5 for refusal"*

> *"No money given to soldiers or sailors (they are helped by treasurers of counties) or to persons begging for losses by fire.   PENALTY:- £5"*

> *"You must hand over books, money and goods to succeeding overseers.   PENALTY for refusal:- GAOL"*

There were 20 such duties listed in all. The first duty of a new overseer was to attend a parish meeting and draw up a list of paupers living in the parish. This was held at Easter weekend. The paupers were paid weekly according to their needs whether they were single, married, with or without children to support. The overseers also saw to ordering of coal, new clothes, breeches, shirts, aprons, stockings and shoes. The monies and care given to the paupers varied from village to village depending on the wealth of the area. It was therefore the overseers' duty to send any interlopers back whence they came. Occasionally vagrants passed through the village, and it was in the community's interest to have them sent on their way. Although the constable generally dealt with these matters, so too did the overseers.

It was also the overseers' duty to care for babies born to paupers, and in many cases, when out of wedlock, identify the father. They would then secure monies from him for the upkeep of the child, and a bastardy bond would be signed. The pauper's medical bills were all paid for. In 1662 an Act of Settlement was made with rules to determine who belonged to which parish.

A person could settle where he or his father were born.
A married woman settled with her husband.
An apprentice could settle where he was apprenticed.
A worker hired for at least a year could settle.
An owner of property had settlement rights.

Throughout the country there was a relatively slow growth of population up to 1750, but between 1776 and 1832 it doubled, and there was a rise in the cost of the rates. As the poor-rate rose so did the idea of a workhouse become increasingly attractive. An act of 1723 allowed several parishes to combine to provide a workhouse for the poor, but Barton decided to build a workhouse in the village solely for their poor. This was built in 1784 in Wales Lane, (on land that had been given by will to the overseers of the poor in 1639) at the site of the modern Collinson Road junction. Almshouses were later built behind the workhouse on the same piece of ground. It was left by John Holland and was described as being off Penny Hill Lane, its name prior to Wales Lane. (The workhouse and almshouses were demolished in the 1960s).

The workhouse was a substantial three-storey building, with the ground floor providing living quarters, the second and third sleeping quarters and workshop areas. The brick building cost £84. It was erected by John Shorthose and David Sanders, but by 1818 extensive repair work had to be carried out.

Barton used the 1781 act to amend the laws for poor relief. The poor were now receiving help in the workhouse and new officials were appointed. In addition to the overseers, a Guardian of the Poor was elected and an assistant overseer; the pay was £20.

The post of Governor had been advertised in a Birmingham paper. From a short-list, a William Pardoe, 35 years, and his wife the same age, with no children, were employed. Pardoe was a gunmaker from Birmingham; he had been in the employ of a gun-makers' company for 14 years but with the close of their business he was out of work. He asked for his normal wage of £30, but the Barton Vestry drove a hard bargain and would pay only £20.

The poor were well looked after in the workhouse, with daily medical attention where needed. A Dr. William Birch submitted accounts that were very legible and well ordered in 1818 and 1821, including charges for such treatments as "draining of abscess, dressing sores, gargles, powders and purges". Treatment was largely symptomatic and palliative, lacking the scientific basis of modern medicines. The diet was adequate if not elaborate, principally bread, supplied by village baker D. Geary, oatmeal, flour, shinbeef, mutton, liver, suet and cheese. The workhouse inmates would produce butter, eggs, milk, fish and vegetables themselves. In July 1820 William

Writtle, nursery and seedsman, supplied 300 savoy cabbage plants, together with seed for turnips, parsnips, carrots, onions, leeks and radish.

The quantities of linen, flannel, mixed cloth, worsted tape, thread and bees-wax etc. purchased from the four village shops show that the women and probably some of the men were busy making clothes. Local cobblers, John Dawson and Richard Chamberlain, repaired the inmates' shoes. The workhouse closed in 1836, and the inmates were transferred to the Union workhouse in Burton. Union workhouses were run on strict utilitarian lines, where paupers were treated more like criminals.

In 1801, by Act of Parliament the Forest of Needwood was enclosed, allotted and divided among the adjoining parishes. By this time much of the original 80,000 acres had been cut down and the ground used for agriculture. There was only, 8,000 acres left, but even more was to be cut down and the land used for growing wheat, the price of which was high at the time owing to the continental wars taking place. The woodland was not entirely destroyed, and today some pleasant areas still exist. New straight roads were put through the enclosed areas. On the road from Barton to Yoxall, on the edge of the village, the area is known as Barton Gate; that is where the gate to the forest would have been. People living in that area as recently as the early 20th century, still referred to themselves as "living on the forest", though there is no sign of a forest anymore.

There was a pamphlet published in 1810, with the permission of the parents of a seven-year-old girl called Catherine Mewis. It was titled *"The amazing Catherine Mewis, of Barton-under-Needwood"* and was the story of a girl who went blind, but could still see on Sundays. Catherine's father was a shoe maker, her parents had married in 1787, and had seven other children before Catherine was born on December 8th 1802. At the age of two, she contracted scarlet fever, afterwards Catherine complained of pains in her head and eyes. At the age of five, Catherine was blind two or three days in each week and had normal sight the rest of the time. But after the 8th April, 1809, she was always blind, except for Sundays. On Sundays she was active and playful, while on her blind days she was helpless and dull. The picture on the front of the pamphlet showed a child kneeling on the floor with a bible resting on a chair, open at the verse *"Lord, that I might receive my sight"*.

Catherine was examined by many doctors who insisted that she was indeed blind during the week, but for some unexplained reason could see on the Sabbath. It was thought by many there was a religious connection and word of her spread fast. Soon it became fashionable for anyone who was anyone to be seen to visit.

Wearing a green silk scarf over her eyes Catherine remained a celebrity bringing many visitors to Barton until 8th May 1828, when at the age of 25 she died from an unknown cause.

Barton in the 18th and 19th Centuries

Barton's fire engine and brigade were in existence from 1820 onwards. In the early years the fire engine which was horse-drawn was kept in a building at the front of the workhouse in Wales Lane, which also housed the lock-up, used by the constable.

In 1828 the Methodist Church was built in Crowberry Lane. The common people would enter the church and be seated at ground level, but there was a balcony where the well-to-do would congregate.

It is known that in 1831 a schoolhouse was built in Barton, though the exact site has not been ascertained, catering for 40 poor girls. Their education was paid for by subscription and the school was run on a boarder system.

In 1835 the first bridge was constructed over the Trent, between Barton and Walton. It was a toll bridge and replaced the ferry that had been used for centuries. When the river was high the waters were dangerous, so the new bridge was hailed a great success. The bridge was freed from toll in 1900, and it lasted until 1947 when serious floods made it very unsafe. It was pulled down and "Bailey bridges" have been used since (temporary bridges used by the army). Several have been used and work is regularly carried out to keep them in good order.

George Stephenson surveyed the route in 1835 for the Birmingham to Derby Railway. The bill of Parliament became an act in May 1836. By September that year Stephenson had been appointed as engineer. 72 bridges and 2 viaducts were needed. Due to his workload he passed the job on to his son Robert. The route they chose was roughly parallel to the Roman road and a few feet above the flood plain of the river. By 1836 work was in progress, and once again Barton experienced an influx of workers. By 29th May 1839 the track was sufficiently ready for a test run. Robert Stephenson took the locomotive called *Derby* from Birmingham to Derby and back.

On 5th August 1839 the first official train, carrying the board of directors, left Birmingham hauled by the locomotive called *Tamworth*. The public opening was 12th August. The company had 12 locomotives; one was named *Barton*, and they were all Stephenson 2-2-2's. The fare from Birmingham to Derby was 10 shillings for first class, 7 shillings for second and 5 shillings for third. From London to Derby was £1 15 shillings first class and £1 4 shillings for second. Barton and Walton Station was built in 1840. It operated until 1957 for passenger traffic, but was demolished some years later. There was also a station at Wychnor, long since demolished.

In the 1850's the licensee at the Shoulder of Mutton public house was Sam Coulson, a brick and tile maker, and described as a 19th century entrepreneur. There were two or three brickworks in Barton. The soil that was removed from the hollowed-out ground on either side of the very top of Main Street, near Barton Gate, was taken for use at the brickworks, (see map page 24) being rich in marl and ingredients for making good bricks. Sam Coulson was responsible for getting the old timber and

Under the Needwood Tree

thatch cottages in Main Street, brickclad. It is said that he would serve the owners of the property with his ales and then convince them they should not miss the opportunity to improve their homes. Today narrow gaps between some of the buildings, showing the timber-framed ends, where the bricklayers couldn't get in, can still be seen.

Around 1850 there was a rope and net works down at the Barton Turns owned by Francis Hardy. It is known rope-making took place in Barton as far back as the time of the Crusades, when trees used in rope making were grown in the Forest of Needwood, specially for the purpose. Some elderly people alive today can still remember the "rope walk" at Barton Turns.

1864 saw extensive work at the church of St. James, when it was widened to its present form, at a cost of £2,600. The church was fully restored and reseated with open benches and could now seat 650. In 1885 the church received a new organ, given by J. C. Grinling, Esq., J.P.

In 1871 Barton Gas Works Co. Ltd., owned by the Lyons family, was founded. It was situated at Barton Turns. The Cottage Hospital in Short Lane was built in 1879, by William Sharp, and in early years operations were performed there. The same year work began on St. James' Mission Church. It was built at Barton Turns, by Lady Hardy of Dunstall. It was built in memory of her son, Lieutenant Henry John Hardy of the Rifle Brigade, who died in Natal, 4th October 1879, during the Zulu War. The mission church was completed in 1880.

The total population of Barton in 1881 was 1,789. It had been rising steadily throughout the 19th century: In 1801 it was 834, in 1831 it was 1,344, and it continued to rise to its peak in 1881; by 1891 it had fallen slightly to 1,775. Other parishes in the area grew much more slowly; for example Alrewas in 1801 had 1,312 inhabitants, and in 1881 only 1,301. A detailed study of the origins of those resident in Barton in 1881 show that many came from places like Alrewas and Yoxall, clearly attracted by Barton's relative wealth and prosperity. Less than half the population of Barton in 1881 was native-born. The existence of Barton railway station made Barton a desirable place to live.

The 1881 census showed there were two doctors; in Barton; one was the well known Clement Palmer, the other was Joseph Richardson who boarded in Main Street. There were two Police Officers, a sergeant who lived in the police house and station in Main Street, known as Peel Cottage today, and a constable who was in lodgings. There was a county court Judge, Woodforde F. Woodforde, living in a house called "Barton Court" on Station Road.

The census provides us with a lot of detailed information on the livelihoods of Bartonians in 1881:

Barton in the 18th and 19th Centuries

Agriculture: 157, including 46 farmers, and others described as farm labourers, cowmen, dairymaids, gamekeepers and gardeners.

Shopkeepers: 28, including butchers, bakers, general dealers, drapers, stationers, confectioners, chemists and barbers.

Traders: 15, including blacksmiths, milk sellers, cabmen, carriers and post mistresses.

Skilled workers: 89, including brick makers, builders, carpenters, joiners, plumbers, painters, upholsterers, cabinetmakers, coopers, sawyers, wheelwrights, saddlers, tailors, shoemakers, horsebreakers, watchmakers, artists, vestmakers, ropemakers, nailmakers, plasterboilers and machinists.

Manufacturers: 4, including cement and plaster, linen, coal and lime merchants.

Brewers: 24, including beerhouse keepers, publicans, inn keepers, maltsters and brewers.

Professionals: 31, including a county court judge, doctors, clerks in holy orders, solicitors, civil engineers, surveyors, accountants, land agents, schoolteachers, governesses, police officers, army personnel, lodging housekeeper, manager of gas works.

Clerical: 13, all clerks, to brewers, solicitors and coal merchants.

Servants: 157, including domestics, housekeepers, inn servants and shop boys.

Semi-Skilled: 86, including bricklayers, waggoners, coachmen, charwomen, nurses, dressmakers, laundresses and matrons.

Canal workers: 9.

Railway workers: 34.

Labourers: 67 (many at cement works and gas works).

Further education: 5.

Unemployed or disabled: 5.

The Cottage Hospital opened in 1879, with six beds, and on the night of the census three were occupied. In 1881 the Post Office was run by two sisters, Anne and Mary Holland; letters were received from Burton at 6.30 am and despatched at 7.30 pm. The Post Office was in Main Street, opposite todays butchers shop, next to where Goodwins shop used to be. There was a carrying business run from Wales Lane, going on Tuesdays, Thursdays and Saturdays to Burton, and on Fridays to Lichfield.

Thomas Russell's ancient endowed grammar school, established in the 16th century, was run by a school board in 1881. There were three teachers who shared the schoolhouse, and they were helped by two pupil teachers aged 15, who lived with their parents in the village. There were two private board schools, both in Main Street. One master ran the boys' school at Radhurst Grange, (opposite Wales Lane) with 7 children of his own and 7 boarders. The girls' school was run by two sisters; at the time of the census they had only three girls boarding. Children were shown as being in school at three years of age, though only 3 girls and 3 boys; at the age of 7 there were 20 and 22. At the age of 10 there were 22 girls and 15 boys, at the age of 13 there were 13 and 11. After the age of 13 there were only 14 girls and boys in total receiving education. The great majority of children under 18 would have left school at 14 to work as domestic or farm servants; there were 48 girls and 28 boys in this category.

There were 5 poor families receiving parish relief, and unemployment was almost unknown; there were only two women described as out of work. The full text of this 1881 census and the census of 1841 can be consulted on microfilm at the County Records Office, Stafford.

The ecclesiastical parish of Barton was formed on 22nd July 1881; Barton was its own parish at last. In 1885 a new school was built to replace the original school built in 1595 from monies left by Thomas Russell. This school still stands in Station Road today. The previous school was said to have been of large proportions. The early history of the school shows that one master was dismissed for "beating children on the head and making some deaf, and frequenting ale houses". Another was dismissed for "neglecting his duties and growing corn on the school grounds". The master's desk from the old school still stands in the church vestry today, with the year 1689 embossed on the front.

Most street names today were different at or before the turn of the century. Dunstall Road was known as Nottle End, (from Nuttall House, Nuttall End). Wales Lane was known as Wales End and Whales End, (from Wales End Farm, Johannes Holand de Walessend lived there in 1509). Station Road was known as Moor End, leading to the flat moor lands at the Turns. Main Street at Barton Gate end was known as Wood End. Barton Gate was Wood End Lane. From Efflinch Lane towards Moor End was Moor Lane. Main Street as it runs through the centre of the village was known as Penny Lane, and the top of Wales Lane was Penny Hill Lane. Short Lane was known as Wilkes' Lane after a local historian, and was later referred to as Hospital Lane. Captain's Lane, named after Captain Arden who lived at Fullbrook House, was known as Greenhill Lane. Efflinch Lane was once known as Walker Lane after the famous whisky distillers who lived at the Knoll. Efflinch Lane was named so because of the hamlet of Efflinch, which was Saxon for heather on marsh land, "haiflinch". Dogshead Lane was known as Pailpit Lane. Green Lane was known as Keepers Lane. Mill Lane led to Barton Mill, and Moor Lane became Station Road which led to the railway station. Main Street from Church Lane to Efflinch Lane was once known as Utter Hill.

Barton in the 18th and 19th Centuries

Bell Lane was known as Fitchet Lane, after Fitchet's Farm that stood at the cemetery end of the lane for many years.

In the neighbourhood of the village are several handsome old villa residences, many of which you will read about later, such as Nuttall House, on Dunstall Road the ancient seat of the Sanders family, Wales End Farm, the oldest building in Barton, its hall dating from 1450, Fullbrook House on Captains Lane, one-time home of Captain Arden, who was believed to be a descendant of William Shakespeare's mother.

The Knoll, off Upper Main Street, was originally built as a hunting lodge; there have been three buildings on the site and many notables have lived there. Barton Hall in Dunstall Road, built in 1724, Silverhill off Barton Gate, an 18th century building, home of the Lyons family, Manor Close off Short Lane, a 16th century coaching stop, known as the Hit and Miss. Blakenhall, off Bar Lane, the seat of the ancient Mynors family.

Main Street is the chief historical legacy of the village. It accommodates a large number of old dwellings and buildings, such as the White House on Main Street near to Efflinch junction, and Barton House, once called Barton Court, the home of the county court judge, Woodforde, in the 1880s, and later visited by King Edward in 1902, during his stay at Rangemore. The Old Parsonage next to the churchyard on Main Street, a building that has had many different functions over the years: vicarage, shops, post office, flats and now restored to a fine house.

The Old Vicarage on Church Lane that was first built in 1670. Radhurst Grange opposite Wales Lane junction, which was a boys' private boarding school. Castle House on Station Road that was once the Grove, home of Miss Holland, last of the Holland family in Barton. Main Street's shops, the black and white timber buildings, the public houses, all wonderful old buildings, too many to mention, but all there to see.

Some old buildings have gone. These include: the workhouse off Wales Lane, Barton's Mill, The 'Flitch of Bacon' public house, the almshouses, Brummagem Row, and Holland House, the ancient seat of the Holland family, that stood on Station Road and was once visited by the legendary cricketer, W. G. Grace, who had tea with the Hollands.

Chapter Four

ALL OUR YESTERDAYS

*(a compilation of newspaper snippets from the scrapbook of
Dr. Ambrose Palmer of Barton. From newspapers in 1895 to 1911)*

LOOKING back to our yesteryears can be very rewarding. Turning back the pages of time can give a great deal of pleasure, and reading from the newspaper cuttings in Dr. Palmer's scrapbook is no exception. Doctor Ambrose Henry Palmer was one of seven children of the Barton surgeon Dr. Clement Palmer. He served on the first parish council elected on 31st December 1894. The family lived in the Gower House in Dunstall road, opposite Palmer close which was named after him. The yellowing strips of press cuttings contain a wealth of information of how life was in Barton at the turn of the century.

Sadly, Dr. Palmer was killed in the First World War, but we are fortunate that his scrapbook survived. It was presented to the Parish Council by the three Palmer sisters, Miss Jane Palmer, Mrs. Susan Lowe and Mrs. Bridget Marshall, in May 1981, a provident care of futurity on their part.

There are numerous pages of local cricket scores. How the gentry of Barton played and loved their cricket! Polo was also a big favourite, Barton was one of the first places in the provinces to take to polo, Barton had its own polo field. It also had a golf course, the club formed in March 1892 with only 19 members; the next year the number had risen to 48. There was a boom in 1894 as membership leapt to 60, but in 1895 a larger course in Burton saw the demise of the Barton club. The polo fields and golf course were on the present site of the John Taylor school in Dunstall Road that was built in 1958.

FROM THE BIRMINGHAM GAZETTE 1895

Barton-under-Needwood, which numbers among its attractions a very fascinating golf course, is a pleasantly situated village, some five miles from Burton. It is an ancient village rich in historic memories and legendary lore, and one of the main ideas of even modern improvements seems to be the preservation of the old world air of the place. The population is largely composed of brewers and people connected with the brewery trade in Burton-on-Trent; those who are not thus engaged belong to the agricultural industry. A large section find infinite delight in the doings of the district council, which, emulating the London council is divided into two parties, the progressives and the moderates. We are not sure what the policy is that divides the members, whether it is the state of the footpaths or the salary of the clerk; but since the members find ample distraction in their work, and afford a good deal of amusement to other people in the doing of it, their end in life is no doubt fully served.

BARTON'S ENTRY IN KELLY'S DIRECTORY OF 1896:

Can you describe a Higler? according to *Kelly's Directory* there was one in Barton in 1896, whose name was Harry Fletcher.

For those unacquainted, it is a person who carries wares about, for sale. The population of Barton in 1891 it records was 1,765. In 1880 St. James's Mission chapel was erected at Barton Turns by Lady Hardy of Dunstall, in memory of her son Lieutenant Henry John Hardy, Rifle Brigade, who died in Natal on 4th October 1879 during the Zulu War.

Principal landowners in 1896:

Sir Reginald Hardy bart. of Dunstall Hall.
Theophilus John Levett Esq. of Wichnor Park.
Lawrence Arden Esq. of Fullbrook House.
Col. Robert Henry Fowler-Butler of Barton Hall.
Lady of the Manor, Mrs. Anson-Horton of Catton Hall.
Arthur Benson of Newark House.
Alex Edward Bird of Nuttall House.
Francis Foster, Mrs. Bruxby and Mrs. Earl of The Elms.
James Church Grinling of Radhurst House.
James Francis Jennings of Barton Lodge.
Miss Lyons of Silverhill.
Miss Nadin of Holland House.
Mrs. O'Grady of The Lodge.
Henry Phillips of The Cottage.
John Reid Walker, J. P. of the Knoll.
G. Arthur White of Barton House.
Miss Yarde of The Crownlands.

Commercial

Dyer's agent, Miss Alice Abell. Plumber, George Allsopp.
Wheelwright, Stephen Atkins. Greengrocer/carrier, Charles Bakewell.
Barton Cement and Plaster Company. Barton Gas Company.
Bakers/Confectioners, Beresford and Arnold.
Cabinet Maker/Hardware dealer, Thomas Ambrose Brown.
Dressmaker, Miss Mary Bunting. Grocer, Henry William Smith.
Chemist and Agent for W. A. Gilbeys wine and spirit merchant, and
Linen Draper, Mrs. Amelia Cole.
Fancy Repository and Registry Office, Miss Carry Durant.
Bootmaker, Francis Woodman. Shopkeeper, Herbert Showell.
Carpenter, George Tunnicliffe.
Clerk to the School Board and Attendance officer, Frederick Smith.

15th February 1897. The Burton Evening Gazette.
The extract of a speech reported to the Editor

Sir Reginald Hardy, speaking of the difficulties of private patrons in selecting the right man for the living in their gift, says: it was not policy to put a fire brand in an ice-house or an old man in a busy and growing parish, or to waste the brains of a scholar upon a lot of country bumpkins!! Forsooth Sir Reginald, the scholar in every parish must not waste his brains on country bumpkins! And this after 26 years of National education, with voluntary schools besides. Fie! Fie! Sir Reginald, what does this mean? I should like to stay longer with "The Squire" but space will not permit.

I should like to picture his changed attitude at an election time, when with hat in hand and eye glass adjusted, he solicits the votes of the "country bumpkins", the "political dissenter", and the "aggrieved ratepayer" to ponder over this.

16th February 1897. Dedicated to Sir Reginald Hardy, Bart

"country bumpkins"

A pratty compliment yo've peed to us poor workin' folk, an' reyther out o' taste belike if yo meant it in a joke; we known if it be left i'th hands of the parson and o'th squire. We'st be country bumpkins unto th'end an hiver nowt no higher. But if it wornt for such as us non worth your while to mend, such folk as yo Sir Reginald ud have no brass to spend. We till yer land, we feed yer flocks, we see yer cattle reight, an' often lie wi' achin boons when we goo to bed at neight. Yo can tramp widow an'gun or foller th' hounds dee after dee, but ivery fraction yo are worth yo owe'n to such as we. A country bumpkin has a heart, deny it them as con, a country bumpkin has a soul, and therefore he's a mon: an' if his blood be healthy, an' if his heart be true, if thems yer sentiments, by George her wouldna wi'yo.

Its over 80 years sin' boney's old guard made their stand, but couldna hold their own against th' English bumpkin's hand: sin' then we've follered th' British flag through many a bloody field, an' yer niver knowed, Sir Reginald yer English Bumpkins yield. So much for pluck an' muscle then, an' if yo mention mind, I know a chap or two belike as isna far behind. There was Robert Burns the ploughman has made a fairish show, James Hogg the ettrick shepherd, Walter Scott was proud to know. (An' he was a greater baronet, Sir Reginald than yo). Bob Bloomfield with his "farmers boy", worn't he a country lad, an' not o very much account if yo reckon by his dad? Naa what we are yo've made us by centuries o' neglect, an' when a mon's no chance to rise what else can you expect? Yet a time is comin' slowly, but its sartin sure at last, when baronets and bumpkins will be memories o'th' past. Another 50 'ear belike Lichfield folk ull see, landowners titled deeds a ancient curiosity. An' naa I've gen yo a word or two from our side o'th' fence, if yo get up to speak agen, for th' Lord's sake talk some sense.

(bumpkin).

1897. Barton's celebration of the Queen's Diamond Jubilee

The proceedings commenced at 7 o clock in the morning with a peal of church bells. The inhabitants throughout displayed flags, garlands, motto's and devices, never in the memory of Barton's oldest parishioners had Barton appeared so Gay. Some of the arches across the street were artistically constructed. After the service in church a procession was formed. The Barton Brass Band, the good intent lodge of Odd-Fellows, the old fire engine of 60 years ago, together with the present one.

The firemen wore their new hats for the first time, the tradesmen with their turnouts represented their trades. The school children under the control of the Vicar, and at the rear end of the procession the famous donkey carriage with its clown.

At 1 pm all the men and youths over 15 sat down to an excellent dinner provided in a large marquee in a field lent kindly by Dr. Palmer. Each participant was allowed a pint of ale or ginger beer with his dinner and three halves afterwards, procurable by tickets. Sports were indulged in upon the polo field lent kindly by Mr. Kirk and a string band played for dancing. At 5pm all the women and children sat down to tea, the former having a good knife and fork repast. The sports and dancing again renewed and at 10 pm a huge bonfire was lighted. A ring was formed around the fire and all joined in singing the National Anthem. The day will long be remembered by the villagers as a red-letter one in their history for the whole populace joined heartily in the festivities. The bells were rung at intervals during the day, and in the evening the amateur ringer rang a meritorious touch of grandsire triples, 336 changes in 13 minutes. Nothing like it had been seen in the village before, every single phase of industry being represented.

Time marches on bringing with it inevitable change. There are those who call it progress.

21st December 1897. Burton Chronicle

Part of a letter written by councillor Joseph Dove, to the chronicle, an appeal on behalf of Mr. Dawson in regard to dole handed out to the poor:

> *"He pays no rent, is given 3 shillings per week poor pay, how much can we expect this old man of 76 to pay?"*

May 1898. Burton Chronicle

Two boys stole a tame rabbit from Dr. Palmer and bathed it in the canal. The rabbit drowned. Police called, after the Doctors groom had chased and caught the boys in Barton Road. The boys were remanded in custody for one week. John Ryan was aged 10 years and Harry Peach was 13. John's mother had taken away his boots to stop him leaving the house, but he had found them and bolted. Mrs. Ryan stated the older boy was the cause of her son's weakness.

A programme giving details of an evening concert to be held:

In aid of the "Waifs & Strays"
    In the schoolroom,
       Corner House,
         Barton
Front seats 2 pence
back seats 1 pence   Children and Dogs half price. !

1897 The Freeing of Walton Bridge.

How many times have you crossed the Walton Bridge? Probably more times than you can remember.

A few minutes and you are over the River Trent and into South Derbyshire. Walton Bridge was once a toll bridge and for the purposes of reference it is interesting to know that the tolls demanded were:

Each person 1 penny return
    2 pence after 10 pm.
Horses and traps   6 pence.
Horse and rider   2 pence.
Cattle   1/2 penny per head.
sheep   1/4 penny per head.

A public meeting was held in the central hall, Barton, on Friday last, the room was fairly filled backed by a small contingent from Walton. Barton people should have a common interest in this matter, and should regard the freeing of the toll bridge to be for their mutual benefit for trade and social purposes. Mr. Mason proposed that the meeting request the county council of Staffordshire to consider the question of the purchase of Walton bridge from the shareholders, in conjunction with Derbyshire, with a view to making it a free bridge.

1899 WALTON BRIDGE

At a local government inquiry held at the Three Crowns Inn Barton, (the Wharfhouse at Barton Turns) Mr. H. Goodyer of Burton represented the shareholders of the local committee who had worked so hard for years for the purpose of freeing the bridge from tolls. The county of Derby was prepared to find £1,500, the county of Stafford £800, and local subscriptions amounted to £1,200.

1900 WALTON BRIDGE

What a wonderful day the 3rd of September 1900 must have been!

"Walton Bridge" is free at last. It has taken 6 long years, at 12 noon the church bells rang out to announce the freedom of the bridge. On the stroke of 12 Miss Disbrowe and Mr. W. Hollier paid the last tolls amidst cheers. Miss Disbrowe then opened the gates and all present flocked over. This portion of the river was formerly negotiated by means of a ferry boat, but owing to the vagaries of the "silvery Trent", and the liability of floods, about the year 1836 the present bridge was erected by private enterprise, the wherewithal of £5,000 being raised by shares of £10 each.

BARTON FIRE ENGINE

On the evening of 16th February 1898 there was a great rick fire at Siddall's farm, Fradley. The farmyard comprised 13 ricks of various kinds of produce. The wind was blowing a perfect hurricane at the time. The Lichfield brigade arrived and a supply of water was found at a pit, but owing to the high wind prevailing, it would be impossible to save any of the ricks, and the brigade were mainly directed to protecting the house and buildings. The 13 ricks ablaze at one time in the strong wind caused a general illumination of the district for miles around. The loss, which was considerable, was said to be covered by insurance; and was well in excess of the £2000 stated.

A large number of fowls and ducks were roasted on the spot, and a cow in a frantic attempt to escape fell into a pit and drowned.

A Barton-under-Needwood correspondent describes the attempt of the village engine to proceed to the conflagration:

Barton has had a fire engine for many years. At one time it belonged to the Alliance Insurance company, but it was given to the village on condition that when the company was interested in a fire the engine should be used without any special charge. The ricks at Fradley were insured with the Alliance, and when the blaze could be seen at Barton nothing could have been more fitting than the old engine, with its new fittings, new hose, new paint and new brigade with their new helmets should have gone to help put it out.

So the engine was dragged out of its shed into Wales lane, but there was a little difficulty: two horses were needed to draw the engine to Fradley but only one was forthcoming. It is true there was another horse somewhere in the village, but it had been working hard all day and had gone to bed tired, not to be disturbed. The one that did come was something of a jibber at anyrate, the only thing that would make it go forward was the sight of a Gold coin and one was not to be had, though it is said that someone offered to guarantee that the coin be produced eventually, and someone else promised a collection be made. But that would not do. It is believed that if Mr. White, chairman of the Fire Engine committee, on the parish council had been there a start might have been made, always supposing a second horse could have been found in a neighbouring village. But Mr. White was away from home and in his absence four things were needed to start the engine. First a set of printed rules, then a second horse, thirdly a gold coin and last of all a man with sufficient gumption to act as a starter and say "Go!". None of these could be had though Mr. David Shorthose, the former engine carer who would always gather a few neighbours and be off to the fire at once, went up and down the village trying to find someone who had some authority or influence enough to save the credit of Barton. He could not understand why the fire should be going on and the engine still standing. Finally, whilst the ricks were still blazing someone was found to undertake the serious responsibility of having the engine put back into the shed, and it is a thing to be thankful for, it might have been left out in the dark lane all night to wreck passing conveyances.

1899 Barton Cottage Hospital

At a meeting it was announced that £44 10 shillings was spent on furnishing the nurses' and patients' sitting rooms, built last year, 1898. The surgery was also added the previous year and found very convenient by Dr. Palmer. Mr. White was thanked for his care of the garden. 60 cases had been treated during the year, 43 were cured, 11 relieved, 4 still in hospital and 2 had died.

1899 Marriage of Mr. J. A. White and Miss Beatrice Emily Nadin

Mr. J. A. White, son of Arthur Robson White of Barton House, was married to Miss Beatrice Emily Nadin, daughter of the late Mr. Guy Nadin of Stapenhill. Miss Nadin was given away by her brother Mr. H. G. Nadin of the Knoll, Barton. The marriage took place at St. James church Barton, with the ceremony performed by the Rev. W. H. H. Fairclough, vicar of Barton. The church was decorated with palms, ferns and flowers. During the afternoon the newly-weds set off for Chester en-route for North Wales. The bride's travelling costume was dark blue voile, with vest and collar of white satin covered with guipure, and a red hat trimmed with velvet and plumes.

1899 Barton Station Accident

Mr. Strong, Barton Parish councillor and one of the oldest servants of the Midland Railway Company, was killed instantly. Mr. Strong, a foreman plate-layer from Barton had been employed by the company for over 40 years, he was engaged in work near the signal box when he was struck by the engine of the "L & NW" train. Dr. Ambrose Palmer was quickly in attendance, but his services were without avail, as death was instantaneous.

1899 July 23rd

Mr. Samuel Archer, one of the last of the old generation of Barton farmers was quietly laid to rest in Barton churchyard. He was 74 but to the last day of his life he busied himself with the care of his cows. He was on his way to fetch them from pasture, when feeling tired he sat down to rest in the cottage of Mr. Francis Woodman, at Barton Gate, and there breathed his last.

1900 Sale of Property

A pleasantly situated and well built house on Barton Green, occupied by Mr. W. R. Mee, at a rental of £19 a year was sold by auction, by J. S. Rowland at the Bell Inn, and was bought by Wm Sharp jnr. for Mr W. R. Mee for the sum of £330. Lot 2 was a cottage at Barton Gate, occupied by Mr. Francis Woodman, which after a prolonged competition in odd pounds was knocked down to Mr. Stephen Atkins for £80.

1900 April

The charity commissioners proposed that a balance of £30 which remained of the money realised by the sale of timber belonging to the Key charity, after £50 had been spent on the purchase and drainage of land in the poor's field on the forest, should be absorbed by the other charities of the township; this balance of £30 should still be retained as a part of Key's charity.

It appears that through a mistake that was made when the Silverhill estate was transferred to Wm. Brooke a portion of the poor's field had been taken to belong to the estate. As the charity lands are by the local government Act of 1894, vested in the parish council, the clerk was asked to explain the affair to Mr. Brooke.

1900 August

The following letter had been received from Mr. Philip Palmer (son of Dr. Palmer) who was in South Africa with the Staffordshire Yeomanry. He wrote home:

> *"I am still alive, and very lucky to be so. I have had a beastly accident with carbolic acid, drinking it instead of port wine. Two of us did the same thing, and the other poor chap died within ten minutes of drinking it, but I happened to have a full stomach and saved myself by being sick, but the other poor fellow could not manage it. He had about a third of a wine glass full, and I had about two thirds. He drank first and did not tell me what it was. If the dr. had not been just passing at the time and given me a powder which made me sick again, we both should have gone. I was perfectly senseless when he forced the powder down, and by the time the other chap got a powder he was too far gone. I do not remember anything else until I was in the hospital. This happened at Lindley, last week now I am at Kroonstadt, where I hope to get better. I shall never forget it. I was taken prisoner by the Boers at Lindley, but only for two days."*

1901 PALMER V BURTON

> *At Burton County Court, Judge Smyly gave his judgment in the action of Palmer v Burton in which each claimed £5 of the other for damages alleged to have been sustained by negligent driving. The judge had come to the conclusion that one of the parties had given an inaccurate account, and the other was under the influence of drink, since there was therefore no satisfactory evidence as to how the accident happened, he decided to give a verdict against each side, each to pay its own costs. It was a sad thing that so many accidents were attributable to drink. The last case he tried before coming to Burton was similar, and he had just come from Bakewell where he had two of the same sort. It was an awful state of things that foolish people in charge of horses and carriages went off drinking. There were more accidents of that kind in this neighbourhood than any other in which he (the Judge) sat. Whether it had anything to do with the brewing of beer or not it was a terrible state of things.*

1901 RECONSTRUCTION OF BARTON PARISH COUNCIL

In 1900 only six candidates put themselves forward for the nine vacant council seats. Chairman Mr. J. Dove, and the councillors were: J. W. Parr, E. Jones, J. Harrison, W. Prior and J. Lyons.

The local newspaper correspondent describes events leading to the reconstruction:

> *12 months ago when candidates were sought for the Parish Council only six gentlemen were willing to burden themselves with office, so that during that year there have been three vacant chairs in the chamber. The ratepayers of the parish would not appear to be at all satisfied with the manner in which Mr. Dove's council of six have performed, for last night at the annual election the whole party were bundled out of power. In their places were elected nine gentlemen in whom the public would appear to place every confidence. Fifteen had been nominated for the nine seats. The chairman announced he would allow time for anyone to ask questions of any who had been nominated. There were a number of questions and all proved to be beyond the councils Province.*

All Our Yesterdays

Mr. Dove opened by asking if Mr. Hardy was in favour of the sewerage scheme being carried out in its entirety. The chairman thought this had no connection with the Parish Council or the election, the vicar said it was out of order, Mr. Hardy went one better, and designated the question as "most absurd" and the questioner as quite ridiculous. Mr. Dove was not satisfied, and being further pressed, Mr. Hardy for the sake of peace and quietness said he was not in favour of the scheme. Mr. Dove had to be satisfied, there was a lull and then Mr. Harrison, a fiery spirited ex policeman, rose to his feet with a vague enquiry as to certain hydrants which it transpired had nothing to do with the meeting. From Mr. Harrison's indignant language one was led to suppose that certain gentlemen had promised to pay for these out of their own pockets so they should not be a burden on the rates. They had failed to redeem this promise and this knowledge roused Mr. Harrison's fire. There were ladies present but Mr. Harrison didn't mind, not he. "Sooner than they should have been charged on the rates I would have pawned my shirt", he exclaimed more than once too. Finally Mr. Harrison appealed to Dr. Palmer "did you not make the promise?" "yes" answered the Dr. "and I would have done so, but you were such fools that you voted against me". The electors smiled. Mr. Prior next held the floor, he had a grievance the rates were too high. Everyone agreed with him; as he could get no one to contradict him he sat down. Then the voting was proceeded with by show of hands, and resulted in the election of the new Parish council to hold office for three years. Major General Fowler-Butler was made Chairman, Dr. Palmer, Vice Chairman. Rev. W. H. H. Fairclough, A. Stretton, F. Hardy, G. F. Oldham, J. A. Hoult, F. Richardson and H. Mason were the other councillors.

1902 ADVERTISMENTS

Wanted, good girl to cook, one who will make a good roast and will stew well.
Wanted, a willing worker to beat and drive.
Lost or Strayed; a heifer, all white except body, head and three legs. Apply Pinner, Dunstall.

1903 VILLAGE DOCTOR

The village doctor was hastily called from the church in Barton on Sunday to a man found in a comatose condition on the roadside by a rural postman who believing him to be resting paid little attention. On his return later in the day he saw the man in the same position and examined him. The postman moved him to a nearby field and informed the police who conveyed him to Dr. Palmer's surgery and requisitioned the services of the doctor.

It was believed he had either had a fit or was perishing for lack of food. Comforts were supplied and there was noticeable improvement. As the poor fellow was penniless and a suitable case for workhouse treatment police conferred with the overseer of the poor and procured a cab for his removal to Burton. The man was apparently an Italian by birth and could not speak English: but he must have had some presentiment that arrangements were being made for his going to another institution for he suddenly took his departure from the hospital before the cab arrived and has not been seen since.

1911 January

Barton's annual parish tea and entertainment party was held as usual in the Central Hall when 306 — a record number — partook of an excellent tea The arrangements were made by the Misses Lyon of Silverhill, tea was served by Mrs Leadbetter, Mrs. White, Mrs. Laming, Mrs Fairclough, Miss F Lyon, Mrs. Nadin, Mrs Palmer, Mrs. Baker, Miss Holland and Miss Nadin.

1911 Market prices

Burton market prices on 15th February 1911:

Halibut 10d. per lb, Plaice 4d. Kippers 1d. cod 4d. Mackerel 1/2d. Shrimps 6d. Lemon Sole 6d. Tangerines 9d per dozen. Walnuts 8d. Almonds 4d. Eggs 9 for a shilling. Butter 1s and 4d per lb.

Old scotch whisky sold by:- Peter Walker & Co Ltd., Burton 3/6d per bottle. Special Peter Walker scotch 4 shillings.

An old remedy for a chest infection:
Heat mutton tallow and apply to chest. Apply a mixture of camphor, mutton, tallow, soot, turpentine and lard to chest. Make an onion poultice by roasting an onion then wrapping it in spun wool rags and beating it so the onion juice soaks the rags well. Apply to chest. Wear a flannel shirt with turpentine and lard on it all winter.

A few comments on the British weather

From 30th December 1894 to 6th March 1895 there was a heavy frost, the River Dove and River Trent were frozen over.

The winter of 1947 was the snowiest this century. Snow fell somewhere in England every day for 55 days and several daily falls were of over two feet. It is interesting to note that at the time of the Domesday Book southern England was rich in vineyards.

Chapter Five

MEMORIES OF BARTON

THIS chapter gives us a chance to look into the recent past of the rural village of Barton-under-Needwood, to try to understand what life in the community was like. It is the result of many happy hours work, seeing people in and around the village, all senior members with great tales to tell, listening to their stories and finally producing them in print.

It was not practical to see every person that has knowledge of Barton's more recent history, the list would be quite exhausting, the interviews were done with people that I knew or was introduced to, and others that it was suggested I see. However, I'm sure you will agree, when you have read it, that it gives a fascinating cross-section of views and memories. It is very important that we remember these memories belong to villagers, some older than others; and whilst we accept the stories and memories as being factually correct, we should not expect that everything stated is beyond question. We must appreciate that these are their MEMORIES.

1. MR. J. HOULT — born 1916
2. MRS. J. HAIME — born 1920
3. MRS. M. REEVES née Woodman — born 1904
4. MR. C. SHEPHERD — born 1914
5. MRS. D. OSBOURNE née Haime — born 1929
6. MRS. M. SHILTON — 1909-1995
7. MRS. G. PRICE née Cox — born 1920
8. MRS. M. JOHNSON née Ottey — born 1909
9. MRS. P. LAMLEY — moved to Barton 1939
10. MR. A. H. REEVES — born 1920
    and MRS. C. J. REEVES née Shilton
11. MRS. F. SCARRATT née Brown — born 1908
12. MR. D. SWINFIELD — 1922-1995

13. Mrs. B. Tovey née Ball   born 1935
14. Mrs. J. Berry, formerly Showell   born 1926
15. Mrs. K. Mycock   moved to Barton 1948
16. Mrs. C. Atkin née Elton   born 1917
17. Mrs. N. Upton née Sorby   born 1916
   Mrs Upton's short stories
      a) an Old Girl's view of Barton school in 1920s
      b) games we used to play 60 years ago
      c) Barton Sunday School between the wars
      d) memories of Christmas past
      e) a summer's walk in the 1920s
      f) childhood memories of the shops in old Barton
18. Extracts from a taped interview with
   Miss L. A. Prior   born 1880   died 1982 aged 102 years.
   taped at her home in 1974 on her 94th birthday by Mr. and Mrs. S. Archer.

Mr. J. Hoult (born 1916)

I was born in Barton Village; my father was a butcher at 46 Main Street, (still a butcher's shop today). His name was Albert James Hoult; and he was born at Newbold Manor Farm, down at Barton Turns in the early 1880s. My cousin, Colin Hoult still farms there today. My grandfather was John Abel Hoult; he moved to the farm from Woodhouses. He was one of the first Parish Councillors when the council was formed in 1895.

My mother was Sarah Elizabeth Sharp; she was also born in the early 1880s but at Wales End Farm. Her father was the well-known William Sharp, farmer and building contractor. He was head of the Sharp and Sons business that operated from Sharps Yard, which used to be both sides of Main Street, alongside the present Metro building and the Bell Inn, and opposite, behind the present pet foods shop and hairdressers. Sharps did all sorts, they operated as a sawmill, stonemasons, well diviners, a funeral service, decorators and builders. The whole job relied on horse and cart in those days of course, and the horses were stabled in Bell Lane, at the back of the Bell Inn. Even the present garage site in Bell Lane was part of Sharps property; it was used by Donald Jones the undertaker. The garage business there today is run by my son and his partner. Sharps did business over a wide area. They employed many men who would all be at the yard at 7 am each morning and set off by horse and cart to places like Armitage and even further.

William Sharp was responsible for a lot of building in Barton and the area. He built the Cottage Hospital in Short Lane in the 1870s; the lane was known as Hospital Lane for many years before it became Short Lane. My grandfather's picture hangs still to this day in the Cottage Hospital. As a young boy I lived at the butcher's shop my father ran. I went to school at Barton School on Station Road, which was considered in those days to be as good a school as there was. I used to serve in Goodwin's shop sometimes as a shopboy for Mr. Goodwin. Today it is the site of 'The Old Parsonage'. At 12 years of age I was sent to Ashby Grammar School, which I didn't like so much, mainly because I had to board, but my boyhood days were generally good times. When I helped father at the butcher's shop we would deliver as far as

Memories of Barton

Newborough, all by horse and cart of course. We had our first delivery vehicle in 1920; it was a Ford Van. There was hardly any traffic on the roads in those days.

I remember my uncle, Charlie Sharp, (William's brother) had a hardware stores in Main Street, on the site of the present filling station. Alty Scarratt's father had the Saddler's store next door; he lived on a smallholding at the back of Short Lane and Wales Lane junction. I remember in those days that Captain Arden lived in Fullbrook House, in Greenhill Lane, later called Captain's Lane, in his memory.

We lived at the butcher's shop until 1932 when my father semi-retired as an invalid to a house in Bell Lane. We were only there a short while. In 1933 my father bought Fullbrook House in Captain's Lane and moved us there to farm. The previous owner was a Mr. Davenport (he had it after the Ardens). He was a retired hotelier from Coventry, and had been there four years. One day he had come into the butcher's shop, and was complaining about the "bloomin farm". My father said "If you dislike it so much why don't you get out?" He said that he would if he could. Father took him straight to the solicitors in Burton, there and then, and signed to buy it.

Well, I lived at the house for thirty years, during which time I had met and married my wife who was a farmer's daughter from Rugeley. We married in 1939. I had carried on helping Father at the butchers as well as running the farm, until 1936 when Father came out of the butcher's business completely and lived with me whilst I farmed. Father died in 1946. In 1963 we moved out of the big house into a bungalow built in the grounds. I am now semi-retired at 78 years of age, and operate in an advisory capacity to my grandson who farms the land.

I remember that Barton had some colourful characters years ago. As a boy I remember a man by the name of Paddy Lindop, who used to dress up and play a banjo in the pubs and other places in return for beer or beer money. He was a larger-than-life character. He wore earrings and had tattoos, he lived in the end house on Whites Row in Efflinch Lane. He later finished his days living in a tin hut on Captain's Lane. I remember that in the 1920s on Boxing Days a group of men in fancy dress would come from Burton and play music and entertain at all the pubs in the village. They called themselves the "Mollyguisers". This custom carried on for many years, and had started well before the 1920s. I can remember Small Meadows Lane was called "Fannashes Lane", and a hut with a tin roof was erected in Dunstall Road for the British Legion, where the Bowls Club stands today. There was a Barton dance band that used to play there called the Boston Band. There were 14 pubs in Barton in those days.

There was a Mission room, at Charlie Peace's house in Brick-kiln Lane, behind the Top Bell Inn, and there was a chapel by the old cement works (the other side of the A38), it was Wesleyan. In Wales Lane there was a Methodist church, and another Wesleyan chapel stood in Crowberry Lane. A Mission Church at Barton Turns was given to the community by Major John and Lady Hardy in about 1870, before my time of course, but I remember these places as hives of activity.

More than 40 years ago I was nominated onto the Barton Parish Council, like my grandfather before me. I served for 24 years, and was Chairman and Vice Chairman a time or two. We used to have meetings at the "Parish Rooms" in Church Lane, (a small, old building that still stands today, though no longer used). Many other groups used the building as well. Just further round behind the church stood some three-storey houses known as "Brummagem Row", long since demolished; but they stood on the site of the present footpath, from Church Lane through to Collinson Road Park. I was very proud to have served on the council for a long time, together with Miss Gilmour, a very popular and remembered Bartonian. I also remember a Magistrate in the village, a Miss Lowe. She was the sister of the late Colonel Lowe: and she died more than 20 years ago now, having resided at Col. Lowe's house in Upper Main Street.

Under the Needwood Tree

My years on the Parish Council were interesting and very enjoyable; I think the dates I served were 1952 to 1976. I remember that one year whilst Chairman, I was instrumental in naming the present Arden Road after Capt. Arden, and the present Fullbrook Avenue after Fullbrook House.

One last thing I would like to tell you was not a memory of mine, but a memory of my mother's that she told me about many times. It was the year that King Edward visited Rangemore. I am not sure of the year; it may have been 1902. Anyway, the King landed at Barton railway station, and all the villagers from Barton were asked to put candles and lamps in the windows of all the houses to illuminate the village and make it pretty for the King's journey by horse and carriage on his way to Rangemore Hall to visit Lord and Lady Burton. You can imagine the scene at the railway station. The village was left virtually empty, as all the villagers gathered to see the King. On his way through Barton he called in for tea at Wales End Farm in Wales Lane where my mother's family lived. When the villagers returned home there was uproar because whilst every one had been down at the station to see the King all the empty homes in the Main Street had been burgled and looted. What a cheek! My mother told me the story many times and I heard it from other elders of the village too during my young years.

Ah well, things change, and Barton Village has been no exception. One thing I often hear is about the old "Hit and Miss" pub, (now the Manor house in Manor Close off Short Lane). Well, I remember it well, but it wasn't a pub as such; it was an old coaching stop. You hit it or you missed it as a traveller. It used to be run by a man known as "squeaker Poole". I remember him as Mr. Poole aged 70/80, a funny little man with a high squeaky voice. Just another of Barton's colourful characters, now long gone.

Mrs. J. Haime (born 1920)

I was born in Tatenhill, where my family had lived for a few generations. I used to come to Barton village as a young girl to go shopping, and later as a teenager I would go to dances in the Central Hall on a Saturday night. I met and became friendly with a young man named Vic Haime. He was a strong and healthy young fellow and we were all very proud of him as he marched off to war with the Durham Light Infantry. We wrote all the time, hoping war would soon be over. And then one of our worst fears came true; Vic was captured at Dunkirk by the Germans and became a prisoner of war.

Vic had been born in Morrey in 1918. His father was a farmworker from London, who worked in the Morrey area, met and married Vic's mother, and they lived in Morrey until Vic was two, when his father moved jobs and started working on farms in Barton and Catholme. The family moved to Barton in 1920.

Eventually, in 1945 Vic came home from the war, he was not a well man; they had done their worst. But Vic was strong in character and he came home determined to enjoy the rest of his life. He was home in the April of 1945 and we were married in the December. We lived in Barton and Vic found work at the Branston and Fauld service depots. In 1952 we took over the shop on the corner of Main Street and Wales Lane. It was called Penny Hill Mansion. The shop, a greengrocery and fish and chip shop had been run by a couple called Neville. Before the war it was run by Jack Cox, who moved to the Main Street shop where Metro stores are now. Anyway, Nevilles moved down to a Main Street site also and had a house opposite Mr. Cox's, they ran a cafe and lived above the shop. It was under the archway, near where the bank is today.

Anyway at the back of our new shop premises there was a petrol pump and a wooden garage building, Vic ran a taxi service from there right up until 1971. He also ran a Minibus service for the schoolchildren.

In 1950 Vic had got himself in the part-time Fire Service. In the early days the fire station had been on Upper Main Street, near where the Christadelphian church is today. It was demolished years ago when

The Cottage Hospital, Short Lane
Built in 1879 by William Sharp, in Wilkes's Lane, it became Hospital Lane for a while before adopting its present name

Main Street, looking west
Note the entrance to Sharp's Yard on the right by the policemen

Under the Needwood Tree

The Barton Free School, Station Road
Built in 1885, on the site of the earlier 16th century school, known today as The Thomas Russell Infants' School

Mr. Simmonds outside his barber's shop in Main Street
Note the Post Office on the left, run by Miss Holland, circa 1910

the new houses were built on Main Street. It was a big part of Vic's life the fire service; for many years, Vic was a leading fireman. In 1971 we semi-retired and went as stewards to Rangemore club, and in 1976 Vic passed away.

As I think back Barton has changed such a lot over the years. I remember when old Mr. Pocock still had his ironmonger's shop in Main Street by the junction with Crowberry Lane, where the Post Office is now. He sold anything and everything in that shop. It was in such an untidy state but he knew exactly where everything was. I remember the saddlery shop, which was in a row of buildings that stood where the petrol filling station is today. One thing that is nice to remember is the contact Vic had with the local cricket and football teams, and today they still play inter village knockout cricket every year for the Haime Trophy.

MRS M. REEVES née Woodman (born 1904)

My grandfather was Henry Woodman; he lived at Barton Gate, and he was a boot maker (mentioned in the census of 1881). My father was Ernest Woodman; he came to Barton with my grandfather in 1871, when only a few months old, from Hamstall Ridware. (Ernest Woodman is mentioned in *Kelly's Directory of Staffordshire of 1900*). When I was born in 1904 my family lived in Bell Lane, and when I was three they moved to Smallmeadows Lane to run a smallholding. It was known in those days as Woodmans Lane, because of our name. The house today is used to run a Books business. My father served as vice chairman on Barton Parish Council for many years from 1925, he was a hard working man, and he died in 1947.

I went to Barton School on Station Road; Miss Stoker was the Headmistress. I remember that there was an orphanage 5 houses down from the school, the house still stands today. It was run by the Belvedere Hospital from Burton and there was a Matron in charge. One of the girls living there at the time was named Stringer; I used to go to school with her. Men from the hospital in Burton used to walk all the way with handcarts loaded with firewood and other provisions that were needed at the orphanage. Later, my mother decided to send me to school in Burton and I went to Guild Street school; I used to go by train from Barton station.

When I went to Burton school my mother had to pay 6d a week. My father had gone to Barton's Radhurst Grange School, and it only cost 1d a week back then. I will never forget the Simmonds's. Mr. Simmonds ran a barber's shop in the Main Street, (a Florist's shop today) and on the other side of the entry his wife ran a little sweet shop. She was not a tall woman, but she was very big and filled the shop, which was stashed full of sweets. If you wanted any sweets off the top shelf, she would go to the door and shout "Herbert", at which point he would put down his cut-throat razor, halfway through a shave, go round and reach down the sweets for his wife, never saying a word and then returning to the barber's shop.

Another thing I remember well is Durant's Lane or Miss Durant's Lane as some called it. Today its known as Cricket Lane, because it used to lead to the old cricket field before Holland Park was built. Anyway it was called Durant's Lane because Miss Durant had a fancy goods shop there (today it stands as the Red Cross hut). She rented the shop from Miss Holland. Another shop opposite was owned by a Mrs. Howard, it was a sweet shop. When Miss Durant died she had been at the shop for many years and Miss Holland never had the heart to collect rent from her during her later years. It seems a long time ago now since the park at Dunstall Hall was full of deer. They used to hunt and play polo up there you know.

At 19 years of age I went to London to work in a draper's shop. I did that for a while and then came back up to Birmingham's Dudley Road Hospital and took up nursing. I was only there 12 months when

Under the Needwood Tree

I was taken very ill with bad flu, and ear problems. In my 20s I had to finish nursing through bad health, suffering with vertigo. Later I went to work in the Potteries looking after the children of a wealthy couple. I had four happy years there, and then came back to Barton. One of the children had Down's syndrome, and I brought him back with me: he lived with me for another 20 years. I married a man named Edwin Reeves. He was Barton born; he had joined Derby's Police before the First World War, then went to war and was very ill with trench fever. He was an ill man but finished his working days at the Branston Government depot. The Reeves family go back some way in Barton (1881 census mentions three Reeves's). You know, I've lived in this house on the Green since 1936. When I think back I remember they used to have marvellous dances and whist drives at the Central Hall on a Friday night; a band from Tamworth used to come and play. I remember Mrs Berwick of the Three Horse Shoes used to run whist drives to raise money for the Cottage Hospital. In the early 1920s she bought the first Orthopaedic bed; they called it the Berwick Bed. They used to perform operations at the Cottage Hospital, I had two operations in there performed by a Dr. Berwick.

I remember the Staffordshire Yeomanry being camped and training on the Yeomanry field (field by the telephone exchange on Station Road). This was before the First World War, they were always there on a regular basis. Then war came, and they were all sent off to fight. Dr. Ambrose Palmer was called up too and lost his life in Cairo. Miss Bruxby was a music teacher who used to run drama groups and the like. She organised a play at the Central Hall where I played Captain Berty Boyd, and I had to smoke on stage; due to my age they had to seek permission from the police. We performed Friday and Saturday nights and a matinee on Saturday afternoon, always to a full house. The Workhouse still stood in Wales Lane. A family named Causers lived in it as an ordinary house. Rileys, a brother and sister, lived in the master's house part. At the front was a shed where the horse-drawn fire engine was kept, and they would take it out on Saturday mornings and flush the drains with it. I was only young when King Edward was crowned but I remember that we had a party on the polo fields to celebrate. "Tea fight" was the name they gave to a party in those days, (the polo fields were on John Taylor's school site). King Edward visited Rangemore, you know, and during his stay he came to Barton to dine at the home of the Whites. They lived at Barton House on Station Road. Anyway there was a bit of a panic because they didn't have a cook, but the Meynells from Hoar Cross loaned them a young lady cook, and the King was so impressed with his meal that he asked for the cook to be presented to him.

There was a Major Lamin who lived at the Knoll. He was the first person in Barton to own a car; it was 1915. Mrs Lamin always used to walk to church on a Sunday morning all the way from the Knoll, and because the Main Street was always littered, especially from the Saturday night, where people would discard chip papers from the chip shop that used to be near the Red Lion Inn she used to pay a local boy 1 shilling to collect all the rubbish up so the Main Street was nice and tidy.

A General Fowler Butler lived at Barton Hall; he was a retired Army General and he's buried now in a vault in Barton churchyard. Every Sunday he would walk up the Radhurst to take lunch with a Miss Lyons who lived at Silverhills. Miss Lyons had a sister that was an invalid following a fall when horse riding. They were real gentry folk. The general rode with the hunt, he wore a red coat, and all the business. When he died his son came to live at the Hall for a while, but later left and went to his other family home in Wolverhampton, and the hall was sold.

Miss Mary Holland lived in the big "Holland House" on Station Road, she was the last of the famous Holland family to live in Barton. The house was pulled down to build Meadow Rise. There were two Miss Hollands originally, and Mary was a suffragette.

In the Second World War, an aeroplane crashed into the roof of Wales End Farm. I heard it happen. One of the young village girls, who lived in the cottages on Wales Lane near to Short Lane, was

Memories of Barton

courting an airman. He had been in Barton visiting and was based at Stafford airfield. His mother lived in All Saints Road, Burton. Anyway he said he was flying over Barton next day on an exercise, and he would look out for her and wave. Well it was a Sunday, and I heard the planes coming over. I remember thinking that the plane sounded very low. All of a sudden there was an almighty crash. I ran outside the back of my house and could see the plane on the ground at the back of the old farmhouse. It had crashed through the roof, there was smoke and dust everywhere. The pilot was sitting inside the cockpit strapped in, dead. Apparently it seemed he had come in very low to wave to his young sweetheart, but then didn't climb quick enough to clear the roof. What an awful tragedy! I remember the ARP man and his daughter trying to guard the area and keep folk away.

I also remember Hanford's coach yard. When it started in the village it was a tin shack, opposite the Vine Inn (the Barton Turns today), on the pub's car park area by the side of the canal. There were three blacksmiths in the village, Poole's was by the Top Bell on Brick-kiln Lane, Joey Dove's was in Wales Lane, and Spencer's was opposite the three Horse Shoes Pub, in Efflinch Lane. How times have changed!

Mr. C. Shepherd (Born 1914)

I wasn't actually born at Barton, but close by at Wychnor. Over the years I have spent a lot of time in and around Barton and have lived in the village since 1939. My father was a Wiltshire man, but he came to the Barton area working on the railroad. That was in the 1890s. He met my mother who was a Warwickshire girl by birth. Anyway they settled at Wychnor, and that's where I went to school, a little building next to the church. The most children that ever attended was 26. We used to come to Barton all the time to shop and see friends. I worked on a few farms in the area for a few years, and then aged only 17 years I got a job as a footman/valet in Stratford upon Avon; this was in the 20s. It was a real posh job, in gentleman's service. I had seen the job in the paper; it was at a place called "Avonbank", working for Colonel William Gardner Melville. He was a retired colonel who served in World War One. They were a well known family; he was a canon at the Trinity Church in Stratford. The family were of Scottish descent, members of the Leslie clan. I went everywhere with the colonel. He drove four different cars; one was a big old Austin. He used to ask me to fill and light his pipe whilst he drove; it used to make me feel ill.

Whilst I was at Avonbank I met many famous people. Winston Churchill was a regular visitor, and when I held the door of the vehicles for him to climb in, he would always catch a hold of my hand and put two half crowns in it and say "Thankyou very much". Sir Samuel Hall M.P. and Sir John Simon used to visit, and Sir Anthony Eden who became Prime Minister. There was an endless list of Foreign Ambassadors. Anyhow when the staff went on holiday each year I couldn't go because I had to go with the Colonel to Minchinhampton in Gloucester to act as caddy whilst he played golf. I stuck it for a couple of years, but come the third year I missed my family so much that I left and went home. The trouble was the depression was on, and there was no work at all. For four years I was unemployed, apart from Army service.

I used to come to Barton shopping well over 75 years ago; it was all fields then, and a lovely little village. I remember Hoults at the butchers, Goodwin's shop, and I got my hair cut a few times at Simmonds's barbers. I posted letters at the old post office run by the Miss Hollands.

Just before the Second World War I lost my mother, and went to live on Efflinch Lane, with my father; we lived just before the old Junction Inn pub (a house today). That was from 1939 to 1946. Anyway there were three million unemployed even in those days, and the population was only 40 million. I did get work eventually with the railways, and did 29 years. I finished off working for the Burton Hospital as an electrician. I remember coming over to Barton Cottage Hospital and taking all the operating lamps and equipment out. They used to perform operations there years ago. I retired eventually in 1979, and I now just enjoy living in Barton. It is where I have always regarded as my home village, all of my life.

Mrs. D. Osbourne née Haime (Born 1929)

I was born at an upstairs flat at the back of Radhurst Grange, on Main Street; that's where my parents came to live when they settled in Barton. My father was from London, and my mother was from Ireland. Later they moved to live in the farmworkers' cottages, on Station Road, the last two on the left as you go out of the village towards Barton Turns, and they worked at Bailey's farm, for Mr. Ted Bailey. There were eight of us children at home. One of my brothers became well known for his activities in the village; that was Vic. Vic Haime was a well-respected man. He was a prisoner of war and was very badly treated. After the war he was a very ill man. Another brother of mine was Jack Haime; he worked at the butcher's in Main Street for years.

I went to Barton School, and I remember that we moved to the first council house built in Barton. It was more than 60 years ago, just before 1934. Four council houses were built down the Efflinch, on the way to the old "Junction Inn". When I left school I went to work at Darley's Printers in the High Street in Burton. I was 14 years old. I used to travel by bus; I had half a crown a week for the bus and half a crown for spending money. I was married in 1950.

Mrs. M. Shilton (1909-1995)

I was born in Barton. My parents lived in Wales Lane. Later they moved to a big house that stood where the petrol filling station stands today, Main Street and Crowberry Lane. My father was originally from Stoke-on-Trent; he was a soldier in the 14/18 war. He met and married my mother who was from Stapenhill, and they settled in Barton.

I was shown the Barton Parish Council Centenary Calendar, celebrating their hundred years, 1895 to 1995. When I was a girl there were still a few of the first Parish councillors around. Anyway, one picture in the calendar was of Barton's horse-drawn fire engine and crew, at the Queen Victoria celebrations of the Diamond Jubilee 1897. Obviously just a bit before my time, but I know the man in the photograph standing to the left of the picture, a white-bearded gent in a bowler hat. He's standing with the engine, horses and crew. They are all wearing their new metal helmets which they had just received and were sporting for the first time. He was a man called Charlie Hackett, he lived at Radhurst Grange on Main Street, which still stands today, opposite to Wales Lane. Charlie was the owner of both of the horses that were used to draw the engine, the horses were stabled at the rear of his house which was also a shop and coal merchants. The engine was garaged in a wooden shed by the Workhouse in Wales Lane, by Collinson Road today.

Charlie Hackett had two horses, one black, one white. He always drove the fire engine, but never wore a helmet, only his bowler hat, and he never took any part in fighting fires. He said he was fully occupied looking after the horses.

I remember the pub called the Swan, which was where the house agent's is now. It was kept by Mrs. Newcombe and the two Misses Newcombe. When my mother was pickling onions she would send me to the Swan for pickling vinegar, which they sold by the jug. I had to go to the basement entrance, and Mrs. Newcombe would fill my mother's jug for me to carry home.

Barton Fire Service 1897. Crew and horse-drawn engine

Pictured during the Jubilee celebrations for Queen Victoria, in Main Street. Allsopp's was on the corner of Crowberry Lane. The men wearing their new helmets for the first time

The Hackett Brothers

of Hackett's Farm; the brothers enjoyed much success with their heavy show horses

Under the Needwood Tree

The Old Workhouse, Wales Lane
Note the shed at the front and left, where the fire-engine was kept; the part on the front and right was the lock-up. It was demolished in the 60's to build Collinson Road

'Upper' Main Street, looking west
Note Cox's stores on the left at the junction with Wales Lane

Memories of Barton

Mr. Dove was a blacksmith; he was on the Parish Council for a time. He was a very kind man and loved children; he made metal hoops for the boys to bowl along with a stick, and we would love to stand by the open window of his forge on the corner of Wales Lane, and smell the horses. He always wore a white baker's hat instead of a cap while he was working!

The other blacksmith's shop was owned by Mr. Spencer; that was by the Three Horseshoes pub. Mr. Spencer mended ploughs rather than shoe horses. There was also Mr. Ottey at Barton Gate who was a wheelwright.

I remember being sent to the house of Mr. White J. P. who was known behind his back as "Pa white"! he gave a letter of dispensation to any mother who did not wish to have her child vaccinated for smallpox. My mother did not want to have my sister vaccinated, and I was sent to ask for the note; he wrote it at a small table in the hall. I was about ten years old then. Many years later one of my sons was to live at that house in Station Road, and it felt very strange going inside after all those years.

MRS. G. PRICE née Cox (born 1920)

My mother's side go way back in Barton's history. My mother was a Barton girl, Hannah Roberts; she was born in Barton in 1893. Her father (my grandfather) was William Roberts; his family were Barton people, and he worked as a plumber. My great grandfather was Thomas Roberts, an old Barton farmer, and his wife was a midwife.

My grandfather, William Roberts the plumber, lived on Upper Main Street near to Whetton's old yard that stands empty today. I can remember that Showell's Bakery shop stood opposite there, and the fire engine was brought up to be housed nearby. It had previously been kept down at the workhouse. My grandfather was a part-time fireman in those days, when it was horse-drawn. When the engine was called out the horses would have to be fetched from Small Meadows Lane, right the other end of the village.

My mother went to Barton school, and later she kept house for a Mr. Dugmore, in Main Street, near to where the butchers shop is today. Mr. Dugmore had been a shop walker in London, like security and supervisor in one. When the First World War arrived Mother went to work at the Branston Government depot, making shells and other war items. My parents met at the gamekeeper's place at Dunstall; they got wed and went to live in Chepstow in Wales.

My parents came home to Barton to have me, and in 1921 they took the shop on the corner of Wales Lane and Upper Main Street; it was called "Penny Hill Mansion". (Today it is a guesthouse named "Threeways") It had been open previously as a shop but then stood empty for a few years. Anyway my father opened "Jack Cox's" greengrocer's store and chip shop there. In 1935 we left those premises and moved to a shop right in the middle of the village main street. (Today it is called Metro Stores) Cox's store was there under my fathers direction until 1965. I worked hard to help my father we sold all sorts, groceries, fish and rabbits. A Mr and Mrs Stan Clarke bought the business from my father, and they employed a Mr. Arthur Reeves as a manager. Arthur later bought the shop and ran it up until the early 1980s, when it became Metro discount store.

Back in the 1920s I remember the very early steam lorry, that was owned by Greensmith's flour mills; they used to deliver flour to Showell's Bakery, and Collin's bakery in the main street. They used to stoke up the fire underneath to get it running; as kids we were fascinated to stand and watch the fiery monster spitting out cinders onto the road.

In the Second World War, Barton's Home Guard used to meet in a long room at the back of Roy Parish's shop in Main Street; in those days it was the back of Sharpes Yard. My father was the quartermaster sergeant. They used to patrol as far as Wychnor Bridges, and would be out all night sometimes on manoeuvres.

I was married to Reginald Price. He has passed on now, but he ran the Red Lion pub in Main Street for years, and his dad Charlie had run it from pre-1900 until after the Second World War. Between them they served for over 50 years.

Mrs. M. Johnson née Ottey (born 1909)

I was an Ottey, you know. That's an old Bartonian name if ever there was one. When I was born in 1909 my parents lived at a house called the Laurels up at Barton Gate (today named the Cattery). My father was a wheelwright and undertaker; he was named William Ottey. He was born in 1880 at a house called "Bankhouse" at the top of Main Street on the left going up towards Barton Gate. He was one of 10 children. His father, my grandfather, was a shoemaker named William Ottey (he is mentioned in the census of Barton 1881).

My father was busy working with the undertaker's business and wheelwrighting. The brick workshop building he used is still standing today. My mother was from Branston; she came to Barton to work as a maid for a Mrs. Howard, who owned the sweet shop opposite Durant's Fancy Repository on Station Road. She was in service to Mrs. Howard for some time. Anyway, she met my father, and they married, so Mother stopped working for Mrs. Howard. Married women didn't work in those days you know!

I went to Barton school, down on Station Road. Miss Stoker was Headmistress. You know, I used to walk all the way back up to Barton Gate for my lunch, and never thought anything of it. Kids today wouldn't do that, would they? I can remember that you always knew when my father had a funeral service on, the church bells would toll. Father would walk in front of the coffin, all decked out in black with a top hat on; the bearers would push the coffin on wheels all the way from his workshop down to the church. The bearers were paid 7/6 each.

They were happy days, or so it seemed to me; but with the new invention of rubber tyres and motor tractors, by 1925 father was bankrupt. His funeral business alone was not enough to support our family. I felt sorry for father; he must have known hard times, being one of 10 children himself. When he was only 4 he was sort of adopted by his mother's sister and her husband who were a little bit better off financially than his parents and who were childless. People did things like that in those days to help each other out.

When I left school, I went to work at Ellis's in Burton as a tailoress; I used to travel to work on the train, from Barton station. I used to earn 6s 6d a week. By November of 1936 my wages had risen to 38 shillings, but I left Ellis's and was married to Henry Spencer Johnson; he came from Yoxall, and was a gardener in Abbots Bromley. In 1937 Henry went to work for John Hoult at Fullbrook Farm in Barton; he was there until 1966, and then worked for another 11 years at Drakelow Power station until he retired.

Mrs. P. Lamley

I was not born in Barton, but I came to the village as a little girl of about 10 years of age in 1939. My father was a Berkshire man. He was working at Ministry of Defence Depots and in 1939 was posted to the Government Depot at Branston; my mother was working at the depot making army uniforms. They moved to a house on Barton Green; it was one of a row of five "villas", houses just before and opposite the Royal Oak public house. My father was called up to fight and went away to war. We never saw him again; he was killed at war. My mother continued to work at the depot.

When I left school I got a job working for Mr. Bennett in the Post Office. In those days, the 40s, it was where it is today, on the corner of Main Street and Crowberry Lane. Barton's first ever Post Office had

Memories of Barton

been run by the Hollands family, since the late 1800s, in a building just up from the church in Main Street, up from Goodwin's shop. Today it is a solicitors office. Anyway, Mr. Bennett took over at the same premises in 1936. Charles Bennett then moved it to the site by Crowberry Lane where I started work. In the 50s he moved it down the other end of Main Street, opposite Church Lane and the War Memorial; it wasn't long after the war. In 1968 Mr. Harry Spalding took over the Post Office, still on the same site. I remember that in 1970 there was a fire, and the Post Office had to be run from the Parish Rooms in Church Lane. In the mid 70s Mr. Spalding moved it up to what had been Goodwin's shop for years and years, by the churchyard on Main Street. Today it's a house, the Old Parsonage. In the mid-80s it moved again to its present site today by Crowberry Lane, a full circle back to where it had been when I started work in the 40s.

I remember that when I was a girl, Hayden's shop was on the corner of Main Street and Wales Lane, it was a clothier's and boot shop. Today the shop is the Country Kitchen delicatessen, and a clothes shop. On the opposite corner was Drewett's shop, a general stores, and next to it was a Blacksmiths shop, today the shop is Penny Hill Cottage and the blacksmiths just a garage building. Years ago where Wales Lane rose to join Main Street it was known as Penny Hill, and the Main Street was Penny Lane. Later Drewett's shop moved further down Wales Lane to a house known today as Buddleia cottage, and the old shop became a Greengrocers and Fish Shop.

I remember when the blacksmith's shop was still open in Efflinch Lane opposite the Three Horseshoes public house; I used to pass it on my way to school. I also remember Brummagem Row, a row of three-storey cottages off Church Lane, behind the cemetery, on the way through to where Collinson Park is today. I used to walk past them as well on my way to school. Barton was so different then. It was still just clinging on to the era when it was a small and very peaceful village. It has grown to a point today where it is almost unrecognisable still a nice village, but different. It is nice to have the memories.

Mr. A. H. Reeves (born 1920)

My family have been in Barton for a long, long time. My grandfather was born in the 1860s; he lived with his family on the Strand, (Upper Main Street) a couple of houses the village side of the Robin Hood public house (a private house today, opposite Park Road). Grandfather was a painter on the Dunstall estate.

My father William James Reeves was born in the same house on the Strand in 1888. My Father worked as a painter and decorator for Jacksons in Burton. He went to live in a house in Wales Lane, next to the Workhouse, it was called Elm Tree Cottage. I was born at that house and went to school in Barton from when I was four until I was fourteen. When I was only 9 years old I was running errands for Mr. Jack Cox; he ran the greengrocer's and fish shop at Penny Hill Mansion, (corner of Wales Lane, junction Main Street). Jack was also a rabbit-catcher by trade. Mr. Cox taught me the trade and skills, and eventually at 14 I left school and went to work full-time for him.

I remember it was 1936 when Mr. Cox moved premises to the shop in Main Street, which is Metro stores today. We worked together there until 1966, the year England won the football World Cup; and then he retired, Stan Clarke bought the business, and I ran it as manager until 1974, when I finally bought the business and ran it until I retired in 1984.

MRS. C. J. REEVES née Shilton

My family, the Shiltons, have a history in Barton village also. My grandfather was William Henry Shilton; he was born in Barton, and later moved to live at Rose Tree Cottage on Station Road, opposite the school. My grandfather worked for the Council, as a Navvy, on the road gangs.

Under the Needwood Tree

My father was Thomas Shilton, born 1901 in Rose Tree Cottage he was a foreman at the Marmite factory in Burton. I went to Barton school. The head was a Mr. Ashton; before him it had been a Mr. Harry Hamilton. My brother was Ken Shilton; he ran the Barton Post Office in the 50s/60s when it was opposite Church Lane, and the War Memorial. Our landlord was a well-known old lady known as Pearly Peace. Pearly lived down Brick-kiln Lane behind the Top Bell public house, Miss Peace was quite a character, in her latter years she was very ill, and went off her legs, but she used to move about the house on her knees.

Mrs. F. Scarratt née Brown (born 1908)

I was born to a farming family in Draycott-in-the-Clay, who later lived in Wychnor. As a farming girl in 1933 I met one of Barton's best-remembered characters at my mothers house, William Aldritt Scarratt, known by all who knew him as Alty Scarratt. Alty was born in 1888, the son of Frank William Aldritt Scarratt who had also been born in Barton in the late 1850s. He ran a saddler's business, and his shop was in Main Street. The building was demolished years ago now, and was where the petrol filling station stands today. Alty was one of eight children born to Frank and his wife, and when they left school not one of them wanted to carry on the business. Alty was born at the house, above the saddlery. Though he didn't go into the saddlery business, his life was horses when he left school. Alty was well known as an excellent horse-breaker; he also taught many, many posh ladies how to ride a horse. It was his job, and people said there was none better.

When the First World War arrived Alty went into the mounted division of the Staffordshire Regiment. After war-time Alty was a huntsman; he rode with the Royal Quorn Hunt. He wore the red jacket, the lot. I have just remembered that Alty's father Frank also had saddlery shops in Alrewas and Yoxall as well as Barton. When I met Alty in 1933 he was 20 years older than me, but we got on so well. He was by now farming on a smallholding in Wales Lane, near to the junction with Short Lane. I went to live with him at 79 Wales Lane, Barton, to run the farm. We had a lot of fields out the back. We used to milk 15 cows, all by hand.

The house, which had originally been two cottages, later knocked into one, leaving a set of stairs at each end, is about 400 years old. The people who lived in it before Alty were named Aspley; they were not farmers. I still live in the same house today. We farmed together for 39 happy years, until Alty retired in 1972. Sadly he died two years later in 1974, aged 87 years, but he will be long remembered by the many who knew him, for delivering his milk by hand with his horse and cart. We would milk at 7 am every morning, and then Alty would load up and go on his daily delivery routine. People knew him everywhere in the area; he always had time for a chat and a smile, and a peck on the cheek for all the ladies. I always had a special affection for all our cows; they were like members of the family. Alty looked after them well, but when he went on his rounds I would always go out and give them some more feed and bedding; they were probably the most pampered cows in the area. When Alty eventually finished his milk delivery round he sold it to one of the milk firms in Burton.

When there were celebrations or fundraising events organised in the village, Alty was one of the characters who was always in the thick of it. There are many photographs of him around in fancy dress, up to all sorts. A wonderful man, long gone but not forgotten.

Mr. D. Swinfield (1922-1995)

Swinfields have lived in Barton and the surrounding area for centuries. When Barton's church was built in the 1500s a Swinfield was recorded as having helped to build it. Oh yes, it was Swinfield, Shorthose and Hardwick that built it alright. I'm a Bartonian but I wasn't actually born here, not quite.

Memories of Barton

Barton Gate looking towards the 'Top Bell'
Once known as Wood End Lane; people in this area as recently as the early 20th century still referred to it as "living on the Forest"

A postman in Main Street
A view of Main Street before the Co-op shop was built

Under the Needwood Tree

Mr. Scarratt Snr. at his Saddlery Shop
A turn of the century picture.
The shop stood on the site of today's
petrol filling station forecourt in Main Street

Alty Scarratt dressed as a nurse at an event in Barton
It is thought this scene was either the coronation celebration of King George VI in 1937
or a wartime fund-raising event for the Red Cross in 1939

Memories of Barton

My mother was from the village but when I arrived she was living in Leeds where she had met my father whilst she was at medical college, it was 1922. Anyway, it wasn't for long before they moved to Barton, I was barely one year old. My mothers side were Elsiebrooks; they have a long history in Barton too. My grandmother was a midwife in Barton in the 1880s; she was an Elsiebrook. Swinfield is of Danish origin, you know; it comes from swine field. Of course, the Danes were all around this area if you go back far enough in history. My grandfather Swinfield worked at Spencer's blacksmith's shop, on the corner of Efflinch Lane and Main Street (the building still stands today; it is a garage for the Redhouse). He worked there for many years, and on the other side of the road, in the small cottage alongside the Three Horse Shoes pub, was a cobbler's shop, and my godmother worked in there; her name was Welbourne.

Barton has a lot of interesting history, you know. I've always taken an interest in that, all of my life. Sir Robert Peel was at the Knoll you know, The Corn Laws were signed and sealed there in 1882 anyway it's on the deeds about the corn laws being repealed. At the Knoll were the famous "Walkers" of Walker's Brewery, they had it for a number of years, the whisky distillers. Yes there's a lot of interesting things that a lot of people never heard of. In the 1800s the house in Station Road called Barton Court was actually run as a courthouse.

People talk about the old Barton railway station, but there were two stations, you know. There was the main Barton and Walton station, then there was the Wychnor station as well. There were 17 pubs in the village years ago. People forget some of them as years go by, but apart from the seven pubs open today, down at the Turns was the Three Crowns and the Railway, on the A38 used to be the Flitch of Bacon and the New Inn (by Heathcoats Nurseries) the Manchester Arms and the Snake with Two Heads were side by side in Wales Lane, The Hit and Miss was off Short Lane (Manor Close) the Robin Hood was on Main Street opposite Park Road, the Junction Inn was down the efflinch, and the White Swan was on Main Street, opposite the church. Did you know there used to be a brewery in Barton? In the 1700s Collinson's Brewery was in Wales Lane; the outbuildings are still standing today. Collinson's Park was used as hop fields.

I remember the Workhouse well before it was pulled down, it stood on the corner of Wales Lane and Collinson Road. It dated back to the 1700s also. There was a lock-up attached to it where the churchwardens would lock up criminals, rogues and vagabonds. There was a brick shed at the side where the horse-drawn fire engine was kept.

Still on Wales Lane, there was a man lived in some old Cottages there called Henry Whapples; Henry was a survivor of the *Titanic* you know. As a young man he was on board the *Titanic* on his way to start a new life in Canada. I don't know if he ever made it to Canada or not, but he certainly lived in Barton afterwards for many years.

I remember that Henry had a speech impediment, and he used to like to go shooting with the police sergeant from the village, a Sergeant Newman. Well, I don't know exactly what happened but for years people used to tell this rhyme about Henry Whapples; "Henry shot at the Yabbit, and he shot the copper's Yat off". He used to speak like that, you see.

Talking of the local Constabulary, I remember that me and a mate of mine, Jim Kerry, who lived in Wales Lane, used to play dominoes at the pub, and one night we played P.C. Challenor. He was always playing, and quite good he was too. Anyhow this night we beat him. Well do you know that next morning at 6 am when Jim was cycling to work at the brewery in Burton, P.C. Challenor jumped out suddenly and reported Jim for not stopping before pulling out of Barton Turns onto the A38. He nearly frightened Jim to death, and there was hardly any traffic on the roads in them days anyway. We laughed about that for years. Jim got fined five bob. Another time when I was a young man home on leave from the Navy I was chased on a cycle by P.C. Woodhall, he was the Yoxall Bobby. What had happened was that I had gone to a dance at Yoxall, and whilst I was inside someone stole the lights off my bike. Anyway I'm cycling through Yoxall, miles away in thought, suddenly I heard "Stop in the name of the Law!" Well, I looked round and in the dark could just make out that it was P.C. Woodhall, a great figure of a man cycling for all he was worth after me. Now I had to be back at ship next day and I had a good lead on him, so hoping he wouldn't be able to see who I was I decided to make a dash for it. Well, do you know, he cycled all the way up Town Hill and all along Woodhouses with his cape flying in the wind. He was a fearsome sight, and every now and again he would shout "Stop in the name of the Law!" At one point he got quite close, and as he shouted it I shouted back "Sorry, can't stop. I'm in a hurry" and cycled like hell. I did manage to give him the slip once in the village, but I was totally exhausted. Many times in years later I felt I should confess all to P.C. Woodhall but in the end I never dared to.

Yes, Barton has a lot of interesting history; Sir Geoffrey Arden lived in Barton, you know, at Fullbrook House, Captains Lane was named after him. The area opposite the Royal Oak pub on The Green was known as Keepers End; down Dunstall Road was known as Nuttall End, after Nuttall House; and down Station Road was known as Moor End, because the flatlands down by the Roman Road, now the A38, were boggy moor areas. Dogshead Lane was known as Pailpit Lane. Barton Turns used to be known as Barton Turnings, because the Canal stopped there years ago and the barges would have to turn around to go back. I once found a 1772 Irish halfpenny down at Wychnor; I guess it must have been lost by one of the Irish navvies that built the canal. Yes, it's an interesting old area, Barton and district. Did you know that it was Oliver Cromwell who knocked the top off of Wychnor Church? No? not many others do either.

One night, when I was a young man, I had been for a drink with some friends in the Shoulder of Mutton pub, and old Billy Shorthouse had been in there. He was a right character. He stuttered a bit, and he used to sing for his beer in the pub. One of his favourites was "South of the border down Exeter way", he used to have everyone in stitches. I think that he thought it really went Exeter way and not Mexico way. Anyhow, he had been in and sung for his supper; it was chucking-out time and it was a real black winter's night. Now Bill, lived with his mother and dad on Wales Lane in a cottage somewhere opposite Alty Scarratt's. So he used to cut through the churchyard and would go along the gulley behind the almshouses and the workhouse and come out in Wales Lane, there was no Collinson Park in those days. So he's cutting through, but what he didn't realise was that old Walter Goodwin, (of Goodwin's shop by the churchyard, called the Old Parsonage today) had been delivering his milk in hand-held milk cans, at all hours of the day as usual. He had a smallholding there as well as the shop. Anyway he had been delivering in Church Lane and was cutting back through the churchyard in the pitch dark, and went to walk through the gate in his wall, which is still there today, and he fell straight into a fresh dug grave that hadn't been boarded over properly. Well he's lying there, moaning and clanking his cans, just as Bill, known to all as Barton Bill, got there, and he moaned out to Bill to give him a hand to get out, reaching an arm up. Well!! old Barton Bill flew out of the churchyard, shouting and white as a sheet; thought he'd seen a ghost, or someone trying to dig their way out of a grave. We heard the commotion and came across the scene. We split our sides laughing, and gave old Mr. Goodwin a hand up. He couldn't understand what was going on, but old Bill never forgot that night. He was a nice character though. When I was only a boy I remember him because I lived just around the corner in Short Lane with my old aunt, Mrs Tomlinson. Bill's mother used to ask me to run to the Royal Oak pub on the Green for her and fetch two pints of beer, she gave me two pennies for fetching it. I remember she showed me Barton Bill's room; all his drawers had padlocks on them. He had a rockery that he was very proud of in his garden; and he worked for Hodges, the builders in Burton, and sometimes he would bring home a dirty great rock on the bus.

Memories of Barton

Before they lived opposite Alty Scarratt's, Bill's dad, old man Shorthouse, lived at the top end of Wales Lane, near where the Manchester Arms pub used to be, and he was a carrier to Barton and Walton station. You know passengers and goods, he ferried them to and fro by horse and cart.

There used to be a group of old eccentrics that lived in Barton; they all used to meet in the Royal Oak. They were educated men but they started to live like tramps, and they would meet in the pub and read *The Times*. There was Paddy Lindop, who used to sing and parade around the village, all dressed up. He finished up sleeping in an old tin hut on Captain's Lane, where years before Mrs Mason used to serve Sunday and afternoon teas. He built a motorbike, but couldn't start it or stop it; the kids would help him push it for hours and when it got going he couldn't stop it so he'd ride around on it until it ran out of petrol. Then there was Sid Lawrence. He took to sleeping and living in an old hut that stood in a field down Brick-kiln Lane behind the Top Bell pub. It was owned by Hacketts. He slept on straw. There was old Tom, and old Mr. Jones; they both lodged with Mrs King on Bar Lane. Mad as hatters I used to think.

One time, between the wars, somebody dug up the skeleton of a man in a shallow grave down at the Barton Turns near to the Wharf House as used to be the Three Crowns. There was a proper big investigation, and in the end it turned out it was a Saxon grave. It was old Dr. De La Russian that attended the original call to the scene; he was at the Dr's surgery in Dunstall Road in those days.

Mrs. B. Tovey née Ball (born 1935)

My father's family have lived in Barton for several generations. I know that my father's father's father, my great-grandfather, was Robert Ball. I don't know his date of birth but it would have been about 1850. Robert Ball is mentioned in the census of Barton in 1881; he was the head gardener at Barton Hall, and he also drove Doctor Palmer on his rounds in the pony and trap. My great-grandfather actually built the cottage in Main Street which is known today as Peel Cottage, and lived there with his family. The cottage stands on Main Street between Church Lane and Efflinch Lane next to the newsagent's. The house became known as Peel Cottage, after it was used as the village Police house and Office from the early 1900s up until the 40s I think.

The newsagents and the house next to it used to be the home of old Miss Prior. She died in the early 1980's aged well over 100, she used to talk about my great-grandfather building the house next door to her.

My grandfather was born to Robert and his wife in February of 1880. He was Henry Ball, and he worked on the railways in Burton as a locomotive engineer. He used to cycle to work each day.

My father, Thomas Ball, was born on 8th June 1908 and he too worked on the railways, as had his father before him. When I was born the family lived in the house next to the Red Lion public house in Main Street. My parents later moved to live in Winshill, in Burton.

Tragically my mother and father both died in their thirties within six months of each other, from different causes, so I came back to Barton aged 5, to live with my grandparents who were now living at Barton Turns. The cottage they lived in was pulled down when they widened the A38 main road in the 1970s.

Despite losing my parents, my childhood days were wonderful, I have many, many happy memories. I went to the Barton school as did my father, grandfather and great-grandfather, and years later I ended up teaching there, it all seemed so natural. As a young child I remember singing at the Mission church at the Turns. A Mr. Webster used to play the flute. We would sing there on a regular basis. We looked forward to it.

Under the Needwood Tree

I remember during the Second World War the Yanks would often drive through Barton, in long convoys. We children would get very excited because they would throw things to us as they drove past, chewing-gum, sweets, tins of coffee, tins of fruit, etc. In 1945 the celebrations for VE day, Victory in Europe, were tremendous. All the children were given ice cream and bananas. We had never seen these before; it was great.

As a child I can remember my Uncle George Ball was an undertaker, the yard at the back of Metro's shop was his yard, he lived in Bell Lane at the house named 'Croftside'. Mr. Donald Jones was also an undertaker, he lived in Wales Lane. When I left school I went into the Civil Service and later into teaching. I remember a lot of interesting people that lived in Barton. There was a woman called Miss Peace; she lived in a house on Brickkiln Lane at the Top Bell public house on Barton Gate. Her father had been an astute and well respected businessman, who ran a mission room at his home when he was alive. Miss Peace was known affectionately as Pearly Peace. She was the landlady of some premises in the Main Street, on the corner of Wales Lane; The Villa and Penny Hill Mansion, which is a guesthouse today known as Threeways. I think Pearly was in her late 80s when she died in the early 1980s. She had finished her days unable to walk; she was confined to the house but used to move around on her knees, I don't think she had any gas, electricity or water.

I remember a Miss Holland, who lived at the castle-fronted house on Station Road, by the Red Cross hut. Miss Holland was the last member of the 'famous Hollands of Barton' family to live in Barton. Miss Holland was a Governor at the school in Barton from 1880 to 1900, she had a housekeeper called Miss Green, who lived in a house that came up to the footpath on the bend on Station Road.

In the 1950's a Miss Morris and a Herbert Morris lived at Barton House, a brother and sister. The house next door was known for years as Hunter's Lodge, two sisters named Hunter lived there; their brother was a Dr. Hunter, hence the house name, and the Hunter's Lodge home for the elderly in Burton which was named after him. A Major Hardy was related to the Holland family and lived in the big house on Station Road. It was demolished to make way when Meadow Rise was built.

I remember going to the auction and sale at Holland House, all the furniture was placed outside on the field by the school. I remember Miss Gilmour. She was not born in Barton but had a long association with the village, and became a well-known and well-respected member of the community, hence Gilmour Lane. Miss Gilmour's father was the vicar at Branston road and when he died, she moved with her Mother to a tall house on the bend at Station Road. Miss Gilmour never married. She was always involved in local affairs; she was a Parish Councillor, a school governor, she started the Red Cross movement in the village and was well liked by all, later Miss Gilmour moved to Wales Lane, living opposite Short Lane until she died in Barton Cottage Hospital, leaving no family.

I live in Pear Tree Cottage, in Main Street, it is an old house, in 1864 it was owned by a Revd Wyatt and Revd Latham. Later it was owned by Hanfords, who were the coach and bus transport people; in the 1930s they ran a small cycle repairs shop from the house. They had a bus yard opposite the Vine Inn at Barton Turns, and later moved to the garage site further along. I know that my parents were married at Barton church in 1932. My grandfather Henry Ball had a big association with Barton Cricket Club. Back then the cricket field was where Holland Park stands today. The lane at the side of the Red Cross hut is still known locally as Cricket Lane.

Mrs. J. Berry (formerly Mrs. Showell) (born 1926)

I am not a Barton person by birth, I was brought to Barton by an airman that I met and married whilst we were at the same camp during the war. I couldn't have imagined what life was going to be like in the NAAFI, and then as a wife in the village of Barton-under-Needwood.

Memories of Barton

Main Street, looking east

Goodwin's Shop, Main Street
Mr. Walter Goodwin and his staff posing outside his shop

Under the Needwood Tree

A Barton Cricket Club tea, circa 1920

Picture taken in the garden of no. 20 Main Street. Note the assortment of chairs and tables. Pictured standing in the centre is Mr. Sharp of Sharps Builders. Seated centre, at table on right of picture, is Henry Ball, a railway engineer. Seated centre, facing camera, wearing a straw hat, is Donald Jones, undertaker. Also seated centre, facing camera, in a collar and tie, is Mr. J. Simnett, a farmer.

A cottage on 'The Green'

A view of a picturesque old cottage that stood at Barton Green. Long since demolished, this cottage was a favourite of postcard scene photographers

Memories of Barton

I married Eddie Showell, whose family certainly were Barton folk. Eddie's family ran Showell's bakery, his grandfather, who was born in the 1870s, started the bakery business, and Eddie's father, John Showell, who was born about 1900, ran the bakery at 77 Main Street, which was up beyond Wales Lane, on the left going towards Yoxall, before where Barton Park is today. Anyway Eddie in turn helped to run the business, and did so when he returned home after the war, with a new wife.

I didn't mention, but Eddie was born in 1925, at the house in Upper Main Street. Our first home together was on Barton Green in a tiny two bedroom cottage, with low windows and an old brass bed with a brand new mattress, and candles to light the room. Some time later, in 1948 or thereabouts, Sharpes were selling up from the well-known Sharpe's Yard site in Main Street, opposite the Bell Inn. They went to see Eddie's dad, and talked about the future of the bakery and the fire engine which was housed at their premises in Main Street, with their premises for sale being the main object of discussion. My husband came home with a fireman's uniform. The Staffordshire Fire Brigade was taking over from the National Fire Service, the wartime fire brigade, and Eddie had been persuaded to join. The fire engine as I said, was housed in a shed at the back of the old Sharpe's Yard, in the middle of Main Street. The siren was controlled with a button fixed to the yard wall; calls for the fire brigade were directed to a greengrocer's opposite, owned by Mr. and Mrs. Neville.

Eddie's family bought the builder's yard property from Sharpes, and we went to live at the shop and house that Eddie's dad owned at the top of Main Street, no 77. Eddie's parents moved to Sharpes old yard where they built a larger bakery and shop. The fire engine was moved up to the old bakery area in upper Main Street and into an old stable. This left the engine at one end of the village and the siren in the middle.

The calls were directed to me at the top end. What a situation it was, I had to phone Eddie's family to put on the siren, and if they did not answer the young girl assistant in the shop had to run for her bicycle and pedal like mad to go and raise the alarm. This would sometimes happen around mid-afternoon when the farmer next door was bringing the cows up the road for milking.

Eventually I was issued with a switchboard and a siren switch nearby. A house bell system with a switch at the top of the stairs was installed for calls in the night. The men were on a retained status. I was enrolled as a firewoman, receiving £13 and 15 shillings a year for taking calls, keeping the log book, passing messages to H.Q., and doing so many hours a week cleaning. With this and two children, I was kept very busy, I also helped out in the shop. When Eddie and the lads had been called away to a fire leaving his bread delivery van in the street, I would go and carry on with the deliveries.

It was a hectic scene in those days when the siren sounded. Fred came running from the farm, Jack and Syd from the butcher's shop, and Vic from the greengrocery. The Officer-in-Charge was last to arrive because he was the manager at the Co-op, which was further away. When the engine went by everyone stopped to look. The man riding in the passenger seat would have his hand through the leather strap attached to the bell, ringing for all he was worth.

I remember that railway embankment fires were common, the sparks from the old steam engines would soon start a fire on a hot summer day. The engine was called out to all sorts, once it was a lady locked in a lavatory. Watching the men run for the engine really was funny, at night time they would be struggling to get dressed as they ran, jackets and pyjama cords getting entwined, but they were always buttoned up correct when they arrived at the fire.

There was a good spirit among the men, and they needed it; sometimes they would be at work all day and then out at a fire all night. They always looked for the funny side of things, one man used to like to tell people he had been in bedrooms feeling breasts all night, meaning the chimney breast after a chimney fire. There were many scary episodes though, where the men faced danger.

By 1966 the workload for the Fire Brigade was growing fast, more house fires, and more calls to road accidents. Big changes were made, and Barton had a new station built and a modern engine installed.

Mrs. K. Mycock (moved to Barton in 1948)

I am not a Barton person. I came to Barton to marry Mr. Mycock in 1948; my husband was retiring and bought the house known as Crownlands on Efflinch Lane.

Barton has changed such a lot, even since 1948. When I first lived at Crownlands there were not many houses in Efflinch Lane, apart from White's Row, our place and a few cottages. There were no street lights, and to catch a bus you had to walk to the Shoulder of Mutton in Main Street. Mr Kirkham was the village policeman. He lived in the Police House in Main Street, opposite Church Lane; today it is called Peel Cottage.

All our fields from Crownlands, which was a smallholding, were on the other side of the road, where Arden Road is built now. We used to rent out the land to a farmer named Mr. Hackett; he kept shire horses. When they built Arden Road it was supposed to be a cul-de-sac. That idea soon changed; now it's all built on. I was very sad when they built all along Captain's Lane and developed it; it used to be so wonderful. Anyway, when we bought Crownlands we bought it from a Mr. Long, but it was known that before he owned it, going back many years a Mr. Troutbeck had resided there. He was an Agent for the Hardys at Dunstall, a well-to-do gent. A Miss Arden of the famous Arden family from Fullbrook House was very sweet on Mr. Troutbeck; they would dine together and ride out on fine days. When Mr. Troutbeck died, Miss Arden was dreadfully upset, and for years wouldn't let anything be done with the house; no-one was allowed to touch his things. (Ardens and Troutbecks are mentioned in the 1881 census and other directories of the time).

My great-grandmother was born in Barton, and is mentioned in the church register for her christening, in the early 1800s. Later she was a nurse, and had a small shop in the village; she was named Harriet Aston.

My husband died in 1970; he was twenty years older than me, so I have been alone for a long time, and that's how I became involved with the Mayflower Club, and that's what I wanted to tell you about. Although I wasn't involved until 1970, it had started in 1962. Before then a Mr. Hopley used Hanford's coach service to organise days out and short trips for the elderly. Anyway Mrs Cook formed a committee in 1962 as an extension of the activities, and it was called the Mayflower Club. Mrs Cook was an American, so with thoughts of the early settlers' ship, the *Mayflower*, and the fact that it was formed in May, so the name was born. The club still meets every Wednesday afternoon from 2 pm till 4 pm at St. James's Church hall.

When Mrs. Cook finished, Mrs. Greenwood took over, then Mrs. Mean, Mrs. Kennet and five years ago Mrs. Pat Smith, assisted by Mrs. Barbara Insley and Mrs. Pat Banks. There are currently over 40 members. In the past we have had many of Barton's colourful old characters, including Miss Prior who lived to well over 100, 102 I think. I remember that Mrs. Cook lived in Radhurst Grange, on Main Street opposite Wales Lane in 1962.

Mrs. C. Atkin, née Elton (born 1917)

I was born in Barton in 1917, in the house in Short Lane, where I still live today. My father was Alfred Elton; he was born in Barton in 1873, at a house in Dunstall Road, called Barton Fields. (The cottage just after the four council houses on the right going out towards Tatenhill). My father was a gardener for

Memories of Barton

A 'Rest of the Village' cricket team 1895

The old cricket pavilion, when the cricket field was along Cricket Lane (where Holland Park is today). This 'rest of the village' team played and were beaten by a team made up of members of the White and Palmer families. Seated on far left of the bench on the right of the picture as you look at it is Alfred Elton. He was first in to bat and was bowled by P. J. White for one run

Scorecard for Whites and Palmers versus Rest of the Village

A. White on the scorecard was probably Arthur Robson White, who was on the first Parish Council. Clement Palmer of the Palmer family was also on the first council, though it seems he did not play in this match

Under the Needwood Tree

Cottages at 'The Efflinch'
A view of Efflinch Lane taken from Wychnor side of the Efflinch, looking towards Barton.
These cottages are next to the marsh lands where heather grows, hence the Saxon name 'Hai-flinch'.
Note the sign hanging outside the 'Junction Inn' public house

Mrs. Simmonds outside 'The Victoria Stores'
Note the many advertisements; Lipton's Tea, Robin Starch.
Colman's Starch, Player's Tobacco, Fry's Chocolate and Cadbury's Chocolate

Memories of Barton

Mr. H. G. Nadin of Nuttall House for many years. Later he worked as a gardener for Major Hardy at Holland House.

I have a wonderful picture of my father outside the old cricket pavilion in Barton, that used to be up Cricket Lane. He is posing with a village team, when they played the Whites and Palmers, in 1895. It was an all village affair; the Whites and Palmers, both large and well known families from the village formed a team to take on the "rest of the village".

The deeds to my house at the Efflinch end of Short Lane tell of there being three cottages on the site; but no trace has ever been found of them. My father could remember Short Lane when there were only a few cottages: a couple near ours at the bottom, then nothing until right up at the Cottage Hospital and the house opposite called Clifford Cottage; then nothing else until you got to the junction with Wales Lane, where you had Shepherd's Farm on the left, and the row of cottages on the right that are still there today, with the "Hit and Miss" set back off the road. Barton looks so very different today.

My father told me that the shop in Main Street at the junction with Crowberry Lane (it is Mr. Spalding's book shop today) used to be a Chemist's. About 1900 it was run by Mrs. Cole; later, about 1915, a Mr. Baker had it, and his grandson Chris Baker, still lives in Barton. In 1900 the Post Office as it is today was a large shop called "Jones's" (incorporating the Lloyds Bank next door). It stocked dresses, coats, men's suits, all manner of clothing. Right by the archway next door was a small bakery called "Mason's" Mr. Mason had a smallholding on Captain's Lane.

A soup kitchen used to be run from some old cottages that used to stand in Crowberry Lane, and from there they used to distribute blankets to the poor. I am not sure who used to run it. I can remember 1922 when Major and Mrs. Laming brought hot cross buns to the school for all the children. It was a regular, annual event. Major Laming had Collins the bakers make the buns specially.

I can remember that the Dower House in Dunstall Road was a home for elderly members of the family of Sir Nigel Gresley of Drakelow Hall. I think it was only for women. I remember a Miss Holland, Holland House was named after her family and my father worked there. Miss Holland however lived on the other side of Station Road at a house known as the The Grove.

Mrs. N. Upton née Sorby (born 1916)

My father was a Burton man, and my mother was from Yoxall; they lived in Burton when I was born in 1916, but when I was three months old they moved to Barton, to a cottage that was first on the right in Catholme Lane. My father worked as a clerk in the railway offices in Moseley Street, in Burton; he moved us to Barton to escape the Zeppelin raids during the war. We didn't move far, but in those days it seemed a long way. My father travelled to work by train, of course, from Barton and Walton station.

I remember as a girl a Miss Prior ran a private girl's school from her house at the bottom end of Main Street, only for six or seven girls at a time, it seemed. One of my friends attended, and she used to tell me that if they wished to use the toilet they used to have to say "Please, Miss Prior, may I retire?" I went to the Barton school on Station Road, where Miss Stoker was in charge of the girls.

My brother, Donald Sorby, was well known in the village as a pianist and church organist. He learned to play the piano under the instruction of Miss Bruxby. Donald formed a dance band with friends called the "Boston Dance Band." They were good; they played on a regular basis in the Tin Hut on Dunstall Road (where the Bowls Club is today), and at the Central Hall, and other local villages. At the age of 30 Donald decided to take organ lessons. He began to play at the St. James' church in Barton he played there on and off for 25 years, and then permanently for 15. In 1949 he helped to raise £2000 for the rebuilding of the organ which saw the addition of a third manual. The organ was then said to be worth £40,000.

Under the Needwood Tree

Donald played at hundreds of local weddings and funerals and many times, having played at a young girls wedding, he later played at the daughter's wedding. I was very proud of my brother; his services to the village were immense.

As a child in Barton, it was so different from today; fewer people, no street lights, cars were a rare sight. We lived next door to the "Flitch of Bacon" public house; it was pulled down years ago when the Turnpike road the A38, was widened. I remember travelling to school on the Barton-run bus service, it was called the 'O. K.' bus, the driver was a man named Earp. At the age of 17 I went to work at Boots the druggists' store, in Burton High Street. Later, in 1942 I married Peter Upton, son of a local farmer. He was a civil servant, and worked at the Branston and Fauld Government depots.

I like to write about my childhood days and have written some short pieces, titled; *An Old Girl's view of Barton school in the 1920s. Games we used to play 60 years ago; Barton Sunday School between the wars; Memories of Christmas past; A summers walk in the 1920s;* and *Childhood memories of the shops of Old Barton.* I forward these for you to use so that I can share these wonderful memories with many others:

An Old Girl's view of Barton school in the 1920s

In 1921, when I first went to the school in Station Road, it accommodated all the children living in Barton. We did not know it as the Thomas Russell School then. A Mr. Ashton was Head master, and Miss Stoker was head of the girl's department.

It was a long walk to school for some of us, and we were glad if we could walk with Miss Brown, who had the privilege of being allowed to take a short cut round the fishpond field and out through the field gate opposite the school. Otherwise we had to take the long way round by the Three Horse Shoes (for some unknown reason it was nicknamed the Drum and Monkey). Of course if we had a ha'penny or a whole penny to spend at Mrs Howard's little sweet shop, we had to go the long way round anyway. When the bell rang everyone lined up at the porch door and then filed into the room where Miss Stoker was in charge of prayers. Striking her tuning-fork on her desk, she would give us the note for the start of the hymn. Then she would read from the Bible, and I watched fascinated as she turned the lovely thin pages. How I longed for a Bible like that. There were prayers again at the end of the day.

In scripture lessons we learned by heart long passages in the poetic language of the Bible. Miss Adamson and Miss Earp were our first teachers in the infant's classes, and our next teacher was Miss Brown. She taught in the small classroom in the corner of the school near to the school steps. In the corner of the room was a gas ring, and every so often she would put the kettle on to make herself a cup of tea. I still remember the smell of that ring. Over a door in one of the rooms was a board with the words painted on it "the quick brown fox jumps over the lazy dog", which contains every letter of the alphabet.

Around the school rooms were friezes which displayed children's drawings, some of which were of seeds such as ash keys and sycamore, pigeons, conkers and blackberries etc, which we took to school in the autumn. In another room the words "Oh where are you going to all you big steamers, with England's own coal, up and down the salt seas? We are going to fetch you your bread and your butter, your beef, pork and mutton, eggs, apples and cheese"; and there were pictures of ships and all good things that they brought. We sat at long desks along the top of which were ink wells placed at intervals, which were filled from a large bottle by the ink monitor. We were given blotting paper, a nib and a nib holder. We had to lick the nib to get it to take the ink properly. The blackboard stood on an easel; we were allowed to wipe it with the check duster, and change the height by moving the pegs. Sometimes a chart was hung over it, copywriting, maps or poems; on the other side were neatly written letters of the alphabet which we spent hours copying.

Memories of Barton

Counting was done on bead frames or using coloured counter discs, and we would chant out our tables. If anyone misbehaved they were given several strokes on the hand with a ruler, or were made to stand in the corner. On hot summer days we sometimes had lessons under a tree on the polo fields, (now the John Taylor School field); and that is where Sports Day took place. We ran the hundred yards, egg and spoon race sack and three-legged race. We loved to go on nature walks, taking notes of the flowers, birds and trees. There were occasional visits by the district nurse, with her black bag on her bicycle carrier; she checked our hair for nits. We had to go for vaccination to the Doctor's, where a group of four scratches were made; we then wore a red ribbon around the arm to warn others not to knock into their arm. On Empire Day we wore red white and blue rosettes and in class drew and made Union Jacks, taking care not to draw it upside down.

On May 29th we made sure we wore a sprig of oak leaves for Oak Apple Day, otherwise we would arrive at school with legs stinging from nettles which other children would chase us with as a penalty. Handwork lesson, taken by Miss Mee, was a favourite. At Christmas time we would make paper chains, calendars and small presents to take home. Sometimes we made flowers, poppies and daisies. We made models with grey clay, and could do wonders with folded paper and "Gloy", paper glue. When the hoppers at the top of the windows were opened by using a long pole, music could often be heard coming from the gramophone; it had a large horn, and was used to accompany the country dancers in the yard. The boy's yard was on the side of the school next to the polo field, and when a ball went over the wall during a game someone had to shin the wall to retrieve it, with permission (sometimes without) from the teacher. Over the wall on the girl's side was the garden belonging to Mr. Shilton, the caretaker, who lived across the road, so if a ball was lost, then it stayed there until it was found.

There was no school uniform. The girls wore home-made dresses; some wore a starched white pinafore over the top. Boys usually had jerseys and knee-length trousers. We had to perform drill out in the yard; we just wore ordinary clothes. Those of us who came from a distance took sandwiches to eat at midday and we sat on the benches around the sides of the porch to eat them. In the corner was an old sink with one cold water tap and an old chipped enamelled mug, so we used cupped hands to drink water, or caught it in our mouths. My sister and I took apples to eat, and some of those less fortunate would wait till we had finished and say "give us the core", so we handed them over.

Mr. White, the school Inspector visited us once in a while, and we all had to be on our best behaviour. Each pupil made out his own report card at the end of term and the teachers filled it in. I still have two reports that show there were eight pupils in one class and four in another, and they were taught by the same teacher. There were a few places at the Boy's Grammar School and the Girl's High School in Burton for those who passed the scholarship examination; the rest stayed until the age of fourteen. Yes, things are very different today.

Games we used to play 60 years ago

   "Pancake Day is a very fine day
   if you don't give us a holiday we'll all run away".
— so we used to sing on our way to school as Pancake Day approached — and we did have a holiday!

Pancake Day heralded the appearance of the shuttlecock and battledore and the whip and top! There was great rivalry to see who could colour the top with chalks so that when it whipped round it made the best pattern.

Of course there were skipping games either children on their own doing "Peppers" or with a child holding each end of the rope for such games as "All in together this fine weather" or for jumping over to see who could jump the highest.

Many ring games were played such as "Poor Mary sits a'weeping", "The Farmer's in his den" and "Ring o' Roses".

In the boy's yard at school there would be games of marbles taking place and another favourite game was putting cigarette cards on the ground and whoever could throw a card to cover one on the ground could keep that card. Cigarette card collecting and swopping too were very popular.

Some of the boys just slid about on the yard to make sparks fly from the hob-nails in their boots!

There were hoops the wooden one favoured by the girls and bowled along the pavement with a stick and the iron one with a metal rod hooked on to it and mostly used by the boys and making a loud clattering noise as it was bowled along.

We could play cricket in the lanes with very little disruption there being just an occasional bicycle or car to look out for.

"Hop-scotch", "Tick" and "Hide-and-Seek" were other favourite games. Sometimes we all joined together to play "The big ship sails through the Alley-Alley-O on the last day of September"— we chanted this, arms around the waist of the person in front, making our own arch and proceeding through it around the school yard.

Some of the girls would be showing off their best dolls which they had been allowed to bring to school and which would be carefully placed on a table in the classroom during lessons.

One thing which I enjoyed was making a "Peep-Show". This was made from a shoe-box, without a lid, over which a piece of coloured tissue paper was stuck around the top of the box.

Inside was a scene either from bought "scraps" or from cut-outs from magazines, etc. At one end of the box was made a small opening to peep through, and to be allowed to do this there was a charge of one pin to see the "Peep Show"!

Barton Sunday School between the Wars

In the days of our youth, when the sun seemed to be always shining, we went, quite willingly, to Sunday School twice a day. The morning was held in the school in Station Road, where we first assembled for a hymn and prayers, after which the children divided into small groups, each with a teacher aged anything from 13 years upwards. We learned passages of Scripture, The Ten Commandments, The Creed, The Catechism and listened to a story. At about 10.45 am we walked in a "crocodile" past the Polo Field and the house where the Misses Holland lived, under the "conker" trees by the Lodge, past the Police Station, across the road by the War Memorial and through the "Kissing-Gate" to church where we sat in pews on the north side. As we sang "O all ye works of the Lord" (which seemed endless!) Miss Mary Holland surveyed us over her spectacles and we dare not misbehave!

During the hymn preceding The Reverend Quibell's sermon we all trooped out of church and went home for dinner. The afternoon saw us back again in church, this time in the pews each side of the nave. Sometimes Mrs. Gilmour would give a talk, one I remember being on a Sunday at the end of November, "Stir-up-Sunday", when she told us this was the traditional time for making the Christmas puddings as well as its more serious meaning. We also might sing her favourite hymn — "The Church's one foundation."

There was always great excitement when a baby was christened, especially if it happened to be one's little brother or sister. The baby would be swathed in a long flannel petticoat, long gown, woolly jacket and bootees, a thick shawl, satin bonnet and over these, a long veil to protect the eyes from the daylight! On Flower Sunday, in June, the church was filled with the scent of the flowers which we had brought, some children brought eggs. All these were afterwards handed over to the kindly matron at the Cottage Hospital.

Memories of Barton

The Sunday School treat was held soon after Christmas in the Central Hall, where we sat at long tables for tea after which there was some kind of entertainment and prizes were given for attendance. Then we went home, each clutching an orange and a bag of sweets given to us as we went out. Mrs. Gilmour taught some of us to perform "Action Songs" and we did these during concerts at the Mission Church. Our mothers made the necessary costumes. There were screens which were pulled across in front of the altar during concerts.

The Teachers' Outing took place in June when they went by special bus. Once, I remember, to Hoar Cross where tea was served at the "Meynell Ingram Arms", after the party had looked round the beautiful church. Another time they went to Swarkestone Bridge in Derbyshire.

We all had happy times!

Memories of Christmas past

No sooner it seemed, had we finished polishing apples and marrows for the Harvest Festival, than we children found ourselves sitting at the kitchen table stoning raisins, peeling apples and cutting up pieces of candied peel for making the Christmas puddings. That candied peel contained lovely lumps of candy which were given as a reward for our work. Not all the raisins found their way into the Christmas puddings either! When all the ingredients had been put together in the mixing bowl we each gave the mixture three good stirs, at the same time making a wish; and the basins were filled and put into the big iron pots to cook on the fire. At some stage a number of threepenny bits found their way into the puddings.

A few days before Christmas the home-reared cockerel had to be plucked and we gave a hand with that. There was great excitement putting up the decorations — mistletoe from the old apple tree, holly from the tree in the croft and paper chains we had made at school, as well as the Christmas tree brought from Burton on the train. We had relatives living at Fradley which seemed to be at the other side of the world! At Christmas time they would cycle along the canal-side to Alrewas and leave presents for us with a friend and we would take ours there too on the Midland Red bus, which I always felt would take us on and on without stopping! It was quite something to see a bus or a car coming along the "Turnpike" (now the A38) then.

Surprise gifts for our mother were made at school and kept secret until Christmas Day. One I remember was a calendar stuck onto a velvet 'pig' and another was a shallow box filled with paper grass and daisies, made to look like a miniature meadow — quite simple things but they gave us pleasure. On Christmas Eve the paraffin lamp was taken down from the beam in the living room and given an extra special clean and filled with paraffin. The hurricane lamp too was prepared ready for when 'Nanny' the goat had to be milked and bedded down, and for those trips to the two-seater in the smallest building down the garden!

We bathed in the tin bath in front of the fire and went up to our beds which had been warmed with the warming-pan filled with glowing cinders from the fire, or sometimes a hot shelf from the oven was wrapped in a blanket and put into the bed. Prayers were said and stockings hung at the end of each bed. "Don't forget to leave a mince pie and a glass of wine for Santa" we said — they had always been consumed by morning. Sleep seemed a long time coming — we listened for the sound of Father Christmas and there were mysterious rustlings as last minute packing up of presents was done.

On Christmas morning those who had been confirmed went to Holy Communion and when they returned someone would play 'Christians Awake' on the piano — not that we needed awakening. We had been awake for some time unpacking our stockings. We found an apple, an orange and some nuts in the toe and there would perhaps be some pretty hankies, a celluloid doll, some sweets and perhaps a pair of woolly gloves. After the cockerel had been put in the oven and the pudding put to boil, we had breakfast of pork pie. Then there would be a few more presents to be opened.

If Great Grandma was staying with us she would 'tut-tut' if she saw we had been given toys; she thought children should be doing something useful, not playing with toys! At dinner we ate our pudding very carefully, hoping to find one of those threepenny bits which would be put into our red money boxes to be spent at 'Pipers Penny Bazaar' or at the 'Staffordshire Knot Bazaar' and perhaps at Tommy Triggs sweetshop on our next train trip to Burton. At tea-time some of our relatives and friends might come and we pulled crackers, sang carols and played party games such as turning the trencher, consequences, blind mans buff and charades and we children gave a rendering of some well known songs with actions, appearing — in costume of a sort — from behind a curtain.

My mind must have been very pre-occupied with food as, when I was very young, I thought the picture at the top of the carol sheet at church was a plum pudding! I later discovered it was a semi-circular picture of the night sky and what I thought were currants were the stars!

This was 70 years ago, but I still remember the feeling of 'magic' which Christmas held for us children.

A Summer's Walk in the Nineteen-Twenties

A sunny day in August during the four weeks holiday from school! What better than to catch a bus at Barton Turns to Alrewas and to take a leisurely walk back again along the turnpike? We alight at the 'Paul Pry' Inn and soon come to the hump-backed bridges at Wychnor which seem further apart than when we bumped over them in the bus. On the canal which runs beside the road from Wychnor to Barton is a coal-carrying barge being pulled slowly along by a horse feeding from its nose-bag as it plods along.

No-one seems to be in a hurry and there is plenty of time as a car passes by to write down its number in our note-books. Our nature note-books, which we always carry with us, are filled with the names of flowers, insects, birds, etc, seen on the way. There are foxgloves, hare-bells, meadowsweet, comfrey and bracken growing in the hedgerow, and bees and brilliantly coloured butterflies flitting amongst them. Over by the canal, dragonflies can be seen darting about between the arrowheads and rushes.

Opposite Dog's-Head Bridge, in Gypsy Lane, are painted caravans with horses grazing nearby and the gypsies making pegs to sell in the village, telling fortunes into the bargain. At the other end of Gypsy Lane we often have picnics and play at 'houses' in the bracken, decorating the doors with white convolvulus flowers. We would catch tiddlers in the clear brook and sometimes gather blackberries or go further to Wychnor Junction and watch the trains go puffing by, waving to the driver and guard, and being excited when they wave back.

On then to the next canal bridge, opposite which is the 'Flitch of Bacon' Inn. The cows are just coming out of the field and ambling down Catholme Lane to the farm to be milked. Mr. Showell with his horse and van, is delivering bread and in the field by the cottage, children are playing among the haycocks. Looking ahead as we go on we see the heat-haze dancing. There are bushes at the side of the road and we hurry past in case a tramp is sitting there, drinking tea from his can and eating a crust given to him by a housewife, as he trudges on his way to the workhouse in Burton.

Just beyond Mill Bridge is the canal overflow where a traction-engine with its load of empty barrels, red hot cinders dripping from the fire-box, is filling up with water as it returns to the brewery. It is not far now to Barton Turns, but first we pass the brickworks with its old kiln, by the little old chapel where Mr. Walker is mending bicycles, past the Railway Inn and the Vine Inn and to the canal bridge where we

Memories of Barton

The Wharfhouse, Barton Turns
*Around 1902 this large building (now residential) was the 'Three Crowns Inn'.
The canal warehouse behind was where the landlord also traded in coal and bricks, etc.*

The 'Flitch of Bacon', Catholme Lane
*Knocked down when the A38 (Ryknield Street) was widened.
It stood alongside the turnpike road just in Catholme Lane*

Under the Needwood Tree

Haydon's Shop, Main Street
*The shop next to the 'Red Lion Inn', at Wales Lane junction.
Inside, it was hard to move for clothing, shopping bags, etc.*

Station Road, looking west
*Note Miss Durant's Fancy Repository shop on the right,
today used as a headquarters for the Red Cross*

Memories of Barton

pause to watch a barge go through the lock. On the other side of the road is the Mission Church with its one bell, where every Sunday Miss Hurst played the harmonium accompanied by Mr. Webster on the piccolo; and, looking beyond that, we see a train steaming into Barton and Walton Station, bringing shoppers home from Burton to cycle home to the village, and bringing back the empty milk churns or baskets of pigeons to be released at the station.

We must turn off now, past the Wharf House which used to be the 'Three Crowns' Coaching Inn, to take a short cut across the fields, along 'Lovers Lane' and so back home.

Childhood memories of the shops of Old Barton

Lets begin at the top of Main Street — The Strand — at Showell's the bakers and grocers, where we went with a jar for loose treacle to put on our porridge. I have never tasted treacle quite as good since! The bread was delivered in a horse-drawn van. On coming out of Showell's shop one might see Mr. Goodhead driving his horse and cab from his yard to pick up some passengers with their luggage who were fortunate enough to be going on holiday to the seaside, and take them to catch a train at Barton and Walton Station. Talking of horses there was plenty of work in those days for two forges, where we used to stand fascinated watching the sparks fly as the blacksmith hammered the horse-shoes into shape.

What has happened to sweet, chewy locust-beans? Mrs. Cox used to sell them at the little shop at the corner of Wales Lane, along with pomegranates and cherries, and raspberry drops packed into cone-shaped bags made from squares of paper. Across the road was Mr. Smith the butcher, and our butcher Mr. A. J. Hoult was further down the street, and opposite a Mrs. Hudson kept a little sweets and groceries shop. On the opposite corner of Wales Lane was Haydon's, there was scarcely room to get inside for the indescribable variety of goods-household linen, clothing, shopping bags to name but a few, hanging outside and inside from the walls and ceiling and on the shelves.

From there it was a 'stones-throw' to Collins the bakers from where floated the smell of baking bread. Mr. Sharp's Hardware Stores was where we purchased paraffin and wicks for the lamps, as well as nails and screws by the pound and all kind of tools. There was Mr. Jones, the men's outfitter and seller of curtain material — Mrs. Brassington sold shoes and Mr. Welbourne mended them — Mr. Scarratt and Mr. Lyons both sold saddlery, the Misses Gregory had a grocery shop on The Green, and Mr. Prior in the Main Street did upholstery. Masons kept a sweet shop and also served teas at their house near the top of Captain's Lane where they kept a peacock. From Postle's a penny would buy a yard of 'baby ribbon' to trim a doll's dress and a postcard could be despatched with a ha'penny stamp bought from Miss Holland at the little Post Office. It was always a pleasure for my sister and myself to go to Mr. Baker's pharmacy to buy a bottle of cough mixture or a tin of Vaseline. On a shelf at the back of the counter he kept a large jar of blackcurrant pastilles and he would remove the glass stopper and take out a pastille for each of us.

A little shop which holds special memories was run by Mr. and Mrs. Simmons — in fact two shops. Mrs. Simmons kept the shop selling anything from whips and tops to health salts. Her husband Herbert kept the barber's shop next door. Now, the health salts were kept on the top shelf, and Mrs. Simmons was short in stature, and so unable to reach them, when she had a customer for them she would call Herbert, who put down his cut-throat razor or his scissors and came to the shop from next-door to reach them down for her. They were a likeable couple and reminded me of Queen Victoria and her Consort!

The Co-op was open as it is today and opposite was Mr. Goodwin's. He sold poultry food as well as groceries, and this was scooped out of sacks and weighed on the big scales. Where the Red Cross depot stands now used to be Miss Durant's Fancy Repository, she sold such things as lace-edged hankies, lavender water, crochet work, embroidery silks, knitting wool and 'rainbow' wool with which we did French knitting on a bobbin with a hair pin.

On the way to the School, in Station Road, we often pressed our noses to the window of Mrs. Howard's little shop and sometimes went in to buy a ha'penny bar of chocolate, a pennyworth of aniseed balls — which made our tongues a reddish-brown, or perhaps to have a ha'penny dip from the bag which hung on a hook behind the counter. How exciting it was to get from it a ring, a whistle or some other little knick-knack.

Barton was a very different place then, but we can still get service with a smile.

The following notes were taken from a cassette recording of MISS L. A. PRIOR (born 1880, died 1982, aged 102 years.)

The recording was made by Mr. S. Archer, a neighbour and friend of Miss Prior, in 1974, on her 94th birthday.

I was born in 1880, at my parents' home in Main Street, Barton, where they ran a family business. (The house next to the Lloyds Bank building today) my grandfather, Mr. Taylor, was a cabinet-maker and upholsterer and ran a flourishing business. When my mother and her sister were young, their father died. Grandmother decided she could carry on the business if she advertised for a man to work for her, doing what grandfather had done, so this she did, and a young man applied for and got the job. He was from Essex, and his name was Mathew Prior. Well, he made a good job of working for grandmother, Marion Taylor, and eventually he married one of her daughters, my mother, and so I came to be. (Miss Prior's father Mathew Prior, and her grandmother, Marion Taylor, are both mentioned in the Barton census of 1881).

In the January of 1888, we moved down to the house I live in now (1974), no. 8 Main Street. (Today it's the Newsagent's shop and house between Efflinch Lane and Church Lane). That's where Father was to continue running his business. It was a larger place, there was a nice shop for all his furniture and things to be displayed, and room for his workshop. In those days there were about 800 people living in Barton. As a girl I remember the Rope Walk behind Mrs Boilings, down at Barton Turns, near to the Wharfhouse, (a cottage industry, ropemaking, a long walk where rope was twisted etc hence; Rope Walk). There were no buses in those days but you could always get a horse-drawn cab from outside the Shoulder of Mutton Inn.

Hard as times were, I remember Father taking us all to Llandudno for a trip out. We packed a picnic hamper full of food. I still have that same hamper somewhere in the house. Mother got a boy to take the hamper down to the railway station at Barton on a sack truck; she paid him but it was a long walk. We passed him later on the horse and cart. He only just made it, I remember the guard shouting him to hurry up, but, you know, when we had got all the way to Llandudno and unloaded our hamper, it was empty. All the food had been stolen! Father was really angry, and to make things worse, at the end of the day my brother discovered that he had left his best (only) coat, at the very top of the Great Orme.

Although Father worked from his shop in Main Street, he also worked all over the area in all the big Halls, Rangemore, Needwood, Catton, Croxall, Walton, Blythfield and many more. One time he was summoned by Baroness Burton, Lord Burton's wife at the Rangemore Estate. She was known to be one that did not waste money. Anyhow she wanted to replace a carpet in an important room, but decided she wanted him to cut out the worn pieces and replace with new ones. Well, it was a very fine, expensive carpet, and Father did not think he could do it and make a good enough job, (he was a real craftsman).

Memories of Barton

Mr. Prior's Upholstery Shop, in Main Street
A view of 'Utter Hill' showing Mr. Prior's shop on the left

Horse-drawn cab at the 'Shoulder of Mutton'

"You could always get a cab in Main Street outside the Mutton"

Under the Needwood Tree

Barton and Walton Railway Station
A rare view of the station, looking from Barton village side, showing the railway station staff at work

'Utter Hill', Main Street
This part of Main Street was known as Utter Hill for many years; it was on slight rising ground from Efflinch Lane junction to the Church Lane junction. Prior to 1890 the area where the Memorial stands today was the site of travelling fairs and shows. Note the police station, left; the police badge can be seen on the wall.

Memories of Barton

He told her so, and the baroness went crazy. "I must, I must have it done, surely there must be a way?" So Father said "there is only one man in the country I know of that could do that job." "Well, who is it?" she said, "I must have him to do it. I don't care where he comes from". Well, it was his father, my Grandfather, and he did arrange it for the baroness. My grandfather left his home and business in Essex and travelled up to do the job. He stayed at the hall, and the baroness was so impressed with the job, that she offered him full-time employment on the staff. She was very sad when he said he couldn't take it because of his business and family in Essex.

The baroness was a great character and she gave my father a lot of work. He used to laugh about one time when she had a carpet fitted by someone else, and she complained to my father that they had made a mess of it, and that try as she might she couldn't get rid of a lump in the middle of the room. It turned out that there was a box of tacks under it.

As a child I remember attending services at the Methodist Chapel in Crowberry Lane. There used to be a gallery in those days, and the posh and well-to-dos always went on the gallery. It's true, a lot of them would not dream of going in at ground level with the ordinary folk.

I was educated at a private school on the Green, run by a Miss Bruxby. Later I was asked to take on the school. I was 19. I ran a school for many years, I was taught and in turn taught how to play the piano. At first, the most pupils I could handle were 15. Cecil Shepherd and Cathy Watkin were some of my first students. (They were mentioned because they were still alive, but elderly). I used to take my students to Burton Grammar School to take their exams, and they never failed. Yes, I knew Miss Bruxby well. She was well known for teaching singing and dancing to all. She used to put on plays at the Central Hall. I never married; I looked after my parents when they were elderly, and an aunt, and later I let people stay at my house as a rest home, and I looked after them. Dr. Palmer would call and see me and say, "Miss Prior I am sending another patient round who needs a couple of weeks rest. Will you look after them?" I always did. One time in particular I did have a manfriend that I became attached to. He was a sweet man, a Minister from Burton, but father found out that he had been married before, and that was that. Father did not want any scandal involving his daughter. Things are very different today. Where my house stands used to be called Utter Hill; nowadays it's just part of Main Street.

Chapter Six

THE EVOLUTION OF LOCAL GOVERNMENT

SOME sort of government is as old as human society itself. How did local government, that we know today, come about. Paradoxically this peculiarly English feature is due, not to any failure to initiate or accomplish a policy of centralisation, but to the fact that the English monarchy was the first medieval government to extend its effective power throughout the realm. To do this the King had to use the local leaders of society as his local agents and to control them by sending his own officers periodically round the country.

The purpose of local government, according to the Herbert Commission, "is to do for people what a group of persons, elected according to law by a majority of the citizens but on election becoming representatives of them all, conceive to be good within the limit of their legal powers". In other words local government is a provider of services to a local community and an instrument of democratic self-government, not a mere agent of the national state.

Roman Britain had self-governing municipalities, a local government of a kind. But it can be argued that local government first started in the second half of the fifth century, after the Anglo-Saxons advanced along the river valleys. The "Shires" developed from these Saxon settlements.

By the reign of King Alfred in the ninth century each Shire had an official called the "Shire-reeve" or Sheriff, who presided over the biennial "Shire-moot" when the Ealdorman was absent. The Shiremoot was the meeting of the Shire's free men for administrative purposes.

Shires were divided into "hundreds", which continued into the nineteenth century. Hundreds were called different names in other parts of the country; in the north they were called "wards". There were about seven hundred "hundreds" in England.

Throughout the Middle Ages each hundred was represented by its Reeve, the four best men and the priest. In each township a town "moot" was held where all the

The Evolution of Local Government

freemen could meet to settle local matters. If the township was fortified it was called a "borough".

When William the Conqueror had transferred many of their earlier powers to central government some boroughs managed to gain charters from the kings which gave them certain privileges and some even 'complete self government'.

One institution that remained relatively unaffected throughout this period was the parish. This had developed from obscure origins as a district assigned to a priest, and gradually gained powers beyond the purely religious.

At its vestry meetings the parishioners discussed matters of common concern and elected from their own number officials for specific duties: Constable, Surveyor of Highways, Overseer of the Poor, each serving for one year when elected and being unpaid.

In 1361 Justices of the Peace were created; they were generally "the landed gentry" and though at first only to administer law and punishment they had by Tudor times become the civic governors of the counties. They were the local government in judicial and civic terms.

During the seventeenth and eighteenth centuries they dominated every element of local social life, civic, economic, political and judicial and very often the Members of Parliament too.

The old system had the merit of making a large number of persons use their intelligence and judgement in the service of government; and so long as the problems it had to solve were those of a simple rural society, it worked well. But it was quite incapable of dealing with abnormal lawlessness or with the new conditions produced by the Industrial Revolution, and after much experimentation an entirely new system of local government, covering both town and country, was gradually built up on fairly uniform lines.

A Royal Commission recommended the Municipal Corporation Act of 1835 which applied to 178 chartered boroughs. This put them under the control of the elected councils. This separated justice from civic authorities and created Aldermen, a quarter of the council elected by the councillors themselves, and made meetings public.

The Public Health Act of 1848 set up 670 Local Boards of Health. All health functions and poor law functions were transferred to Local Government Boards created under the Local Government Act of 1871. Highways and Turnpikes were transferred to the Local Government Boards in 1872. The Public Health Act of 1875 divided England and Wales into urban and rural sanitary districts. This set the pattern of local government as we know it today. It embodied the twin principles of central control of local government through central government departments and local responsibilities for administration of services through elected representatives.

The Shire Counties remained dominated by the Justices of the Peace, who resisted all attempts to control their powers, during the democratisation of the boroughs. But the Local Government Act of 1888, after much political activity in the Shires, established elected County Councils as the administrative organs of country life, in place of the patriarchal rule of the Justices of the Peace. The Justices of the Peace were preserved in their judicial capacity as magistrates. But their administrative functions were handed over to the elected county councils. Each county was divided into electoral districts of equal size with each rate-payer having one vote. All towns with population over 55,000 became County Boroughs. The pressure for the establishment of elected councils in parishes and rural districts culminated in the Local Government Act of 1884, which was passed after much opposition in the Lords. This allowed the creation of Parish Councils and rural and urban District Councils.

The principle of local government established at the end of the eighteenth century was that towns should be governed separately from rural areas. Large towns became County Boroughs independent of the County Councils, while smaller towns became Urban Districts as sub-divisions of the county, quite separate from the Rural Districts with villages and parishes.

Though the authorities administering local government are now quite different from their eighteenth-century predecessors, being more closely controlled from the centre, they have inherited their two main characteristics: the primary control is one of law, and they enjoy considerable freedom as regards the formation of policy and the detailed work of administration.

Parish Councils and parish meetings (all rural parishes have meetings, but only the more populous have councils) are not in a general way subordinate to district councils, nor district councils or boroughs to county councils. Each of these kinds of authority was originally set to administer separate services, according as they seemed to call for small or medium or large-scale administration.

Parish councils and parish meetings have a number of miscellaneous powers, the most important of which, owing to the restrictions on spending powers in the parish, are the protection of parish property and the power to make representations to the district council and, if necessary, to the county council.

The role of the Parish Council is potentially of great importance. They have a right to be consulted on all planning applications; the power to speak for their community, whether advocating or protesting against any course on which their district or county must make up its mind; to lobby district or county councillors concerned; on their own initiative to do anything they think will be in the interest of their locality that is not the statutory business of some other council. Service on these local bodies offers an open door to all good citizens who wish to serve their neighbours in one way or another without having to adopt a party label.

The Parish Councils of 1894/95 and 1994/95

Chapter Seven

THE PARISH COUNCILS OF 1894/95 AND 1994/95

(including the list of Councils throughout)

BARTON'S FIRST PARISH COUNCIL 1894/1895

Listed are the names of the nine gentlemen who formed the first Parish Council for Barton-under-Needwood. The census of 1891 helps us to print an account of each of them, giving, as it does their age, place of birth and marital status. In the "memories" chapter, some of the older members of the village refer to certain members of the council that they remember.

FRANCIS HARDY

A farmer at Fatholme Farm, he was 39 years old and unmarried. We know he did marry later because his son, Francis John Hardy also became a parish councillor in 1938, serving until 1957, he died in 1960 which was only ten years after the death of his father, who lived to the grand age of 95. Francis senior was born in Lancashire, his wife was named Mary-Anne, and as well as a son they also had two daughters. Francis Hardy was the longest-serving parish councillor; his photograph and that of his son were kindly supplied by his daughter, Mrs. Margaret Swire, through her niece Mrs. Nancy Hemming.

REV. WILLIAM HENRY HUTCHINSON FAIRCLOUGH

The vicar of St. James' Church in Barton from 1880 until 1916. Born in Crosbie, Lancashire, in 1894 he was 49 years old, he lived at the vicarage with his wife Constance, two children aged 8 and 12, his mother and four servants. The Rev. Fairclough is remembered by some older villagers. He was quite elderly (71) when he collapsed in the pulpit one Sunday, and was carried home and he died shortly afterwards.

Edwin Riley

Apart from the fact that he lived at Woodside Farm, we know little else about Mr. Riley. He is not mentioned in the 1891 census, probably because he was away from home the day the census was taken.

James Coxon

A farmer of Short Lane, aged 41; he was born in Barton, the only one of the nine that we are sure was a native of Barton. At one time James Coxon was Inn-keeper at the Shoulder of Mutton public house. His wife was named Elizabeth. He died in 1901.

Dr. Clement Palmer

A general practitioner, aged 50 years, and a widower. Dr. Palmer still had four children at home and six servants. In 1897 and 98 he was Chairman of the parish council. Dr. Palmer did not stand in 1900, but in 1901 was vice-chairman. His son Dr. Ambrose Palmer was killed in Cairo in World War One.

Arthur Robson White

A gentleman of independent means, aged 53, born in Yorkshire; his wife was Louisa. They had three children living with them, four servants and Mr. White's sister-in-law. Mr. White was the chairman in 1896 and 97, and again in 1898 and 99. He did not stand in 1900. The Whites entertained King Edward VII at their home for dinner whilst he was staying at Rangemore Hall in 1902. They lived at Barton House on Station Road.

Frederick Francis Foster

An assistant registrar at the county court in Burton, he ran a private day school at Radhurst Grange in Barton. The cost was sixpence a week. Presumably he took over from Mr. Holdsworth when he retired.

Joseph Dove

A blacksmith, 35 years old and married with a son. Mr Dove was chairman in 1900 when none of the other original council stood. He was not re-elected in 1901, though he was a well-liked character. Children used to watch him at work, and sometimes operate the bellows for him.

The Parish Councils of 1894/95 and 1994/95

JOHN ABELL HOULT

A farmer from Newbold Manor Farm. He was not at home on the day of the 1891 census; perhaps he was at market. Mr. Hoult was married. He did not stand in 1900, but was re-elected in 1901. Mr. Hoult's son and grandson, both called John, have also served on Barton's Parish Council.

These, then, were the gentlemen of Barton who undertook to be Barton's first Parish Council. Here follows a list, taken from the signing-in book, of all the parish councillors that followed, right up to the present day. We will take a closer look at the Parish Council of 1994 to 1995, which lists two ladies among them, something not to be thought of in 1894.

PARISH COUNCILLORS 1894 to 1994

This roster is assembled from the Barton-under-Needwood Parish Council Declaration of Office Book that each Parish Councillor must sign when he or she takes office.

31st December 1894

J. W. FRANCIS FOSTER
FRANCIS HARDY
WILLIAM H. H. FAIRCLOUGH (Vicar)
CLEMENT PALMER (Doctor)
ARTHUR ROBSON WHITE, J.P.
JAMES COXON
JOSEPH DOVE (Blacksmith)
JOHN ABEL HOULT (Farmer)
EDWIN RILEY

21st April 1896

CLEMENT PALMER
WILLIAM H. H. FAIRCLOUGH
ARTHUR ROBSON WHITE
JAMES COXON
ARTHUR STRETTON
HENRY MASON
JOHN ABEL HOULT
FRANCIS HARDY
EDWIN RILEY

22nd April 1897

JAMES COXON
JOSEPH DOVE
WILLIAM H. H. FAIRCLOUGH
JOSEPH HARRISON
JOHN ABEL HOULT
HENRY MASON
CLEMENT PALMER
ARTHUR STRETTON
ARTHUR R. WHITE

19th April 1898

ARTHUR R. WHITE
CLEMENT PALMER
WILLIAM H. H. FAIRCLOUGH
FRANCIS HARDY
JOSEPH DOVE
STEPHEN ATKINS
JOHN ABEL HOULT
JAMES COXON
ARTHUR STRETTON

17th April 1899

Joseph Dove
Joseph Harrison
Elijah Jones
James Lyons
Joseph Walpole Parr
Matthew Prior
Thomas Strong

22nd April 1901

Robert Henry Fowler Butler
William H. H. Fairclough
Francis Hardy
John Abel Hoult
Henry Mason
Clement Palmer
Gervase Frederick Oldham
Frederick Richardson
Arthur Stretton
John Stableford Bruxby*

*co-opted on after resignation of A. Stretton 18th August 1902

19th April 1904

John Stableford Bruxby
William H. H. Fairclough
Robert Henry Fowler Butler
James Herbert Goodall
Francis Hardy
John Abel Hoult
Henry Mason
Gervase Frederick Oldham
Clement Palmer

16th April & 5th October 1907

Robert Henry Fowler Butler†
Clement Palmer
William H. H. Fairclough
James Herbert Goodall
Francis Hardy†
Joseph Dove
John Henry King
Gervase Frederick Oldham
John Stableford Bruxby
Henry Mason*

†5th October 1907, *26th March 1909

15th April 1910

John Stableford Bruxby
Joseph Dove
W. H. H. Fairclough
Robert H. Fowler-Butler
J. H. Goodall
John Abel Hoult
John Henry King
Henry Mason
Clement Palmer

16th April 1913

John Stableford Bruxby
Joseph Dove
W. H. H. Fairclough
R. H. Fowler-Butler
James Herbert Goodall
F. W. Hardy
Henry Mason
Clement Palmer*
Arthur William Neville Riley

*28th October 1913

27th March 1917

Henry Guy Nadin
George Cotterill*
Ernest Woodman*

*19th April 1917

The Parish Councils of 1894/95 and 1994/95

Francis William Hardy (1855-1950)

Mr. Hardy, a farmer from Fatholme Farm, was a member of the first Barton Parish Council, elected 31.12.1894

Rev. William Henry Hutchinson Fairclough

The Rev. W. H. H. Fairclough was vicar at Barton from 1880 to 1916, and was a member of the first Barton Parish Council, elected 31.12.1894

Under the Needwood Tree

Francis John Hardy, 1900-60

Francis John Hardy (left) a farmer, and son of Francis William, served on Barton Parish Council from 1940 to 1958. Pictured receiving the Tutbury Rural Council chairman's chain of office from Mr. W. Thompstone

The Centenary Book Committee of 1995 outside Barton-under-Needwood Village Hall

Left to right: Pauline Shingles, Jeff Pattison, Arthur Kennedy, Bill Shingles, Christine Kennedy and Steve Gardner. Arthur, Bill and Jeff were members of the Parish Council of 1994/95. Arthur is wearing the "Chairman's Badge of Office"

The Parish Councils of 1894/95 and 1994/95

8th July 1919

John Stableford Bruxby
Claude Northcote Burt
Thomas Dixon
Joseph Dove
Francis W. Hardy
Henry Mason
Henry Guy Nadin
Arthur W. N. Riley
Ernest Woodman
Colonel Richard Fowler-Butler*
George Ball†

*8th October 1920, †10th January 1921

20th April 1922

Henry Guy Nadin
Thomas Dixon
Claude Northcote Burt
Thomas William Hardy
Ernest Woodman
George Ball
William Armstrong
Edwin James Gallimore
Harry Reece
Harry Hamilton†
Arthur William Neville Riley*
Francis William Hardy‡

*10th September 1924, †14th October 1924,
‡19th November 1924

21st April 1925

Henry Guy Nadin (Chairman)
Thomas Dixon (Vice-Chairman)
Claude Northcote Burt
Frederick Watson†
Ernest Woodman
Francis William Hardy
Arthur W. N. Riley
William Joseph Brandrick†
Harry Hamilton*

†21st April and 19th November 1925,
*31st July 1925

20th April 1928

Henry Guy Nadin
Thomas Dixon
Claude N. Burt
F. W. Hardy
Harry Hamilton
Ernest Woodman
Arthur W. N. Riley
Frederick Watson
W. J. Brandrick

26th April 1931

Harry Hamilton
Francis William Hardy
Ernest Woodman*
Frederick Watson
William J. Brandrick
Francis Joseph Addison
Arthur Willis Rowley
Henry Guy Nadin*
Claude N. Burt†
Richard Sydney Litherland¶

*28th August 1931, †30th March 1932
¶25th September 1933

16th April 1934

Henry Guy Nadin
Francis William Hardy
Harry Hamilton
W. J. Brandrick

16th April 1934

RICHARD SYDNEY LITHERLAND*
ARTHUR W. ROWLEY*
FREDERICK WATSON*
CLAUDE N. BURT†
ERNEST WOODMAN†
THOMAS STANLEY GREEN¶
GEORGE CECIL LOWE‡

*26th September 1934, †27th February 1935
¶28th March 1935, ‡6th November 1936

20th April, 1937

THOMAS STANLEY GREEN
ERNEST WOODMAN
ARTHUR W. ROWLEY
GEORGE C. LOWE
JAMES COLLINS
EDWIN J. GALLIMORE
NORMAN RICHARD STEVENSON
RICHARD SYDNEY LITHERLAND
GEORGE HENRY JOHNSON*
JOHN HARDY†

*27th May 1937, †20th April 1938

26th March 1940

ERNEST WOODMAN
ARTHUR W. ROWLEY
GEORGE C. LOWE
JAMES COLLINS
EDWIN J. GALLIMORE
NORMAN RICHARD STEVENSON
GEORGE HENRY JOHNSON
JOHN HARDY
P. HACKETT
GERALD HAMILTON*
*Co-opted 2nd July 1942

25th March 1943

ARTHUR W. ROWLEY
GEORGE C. LOWE
JAMES COLLINS
EDWIN J. GALLIMORE
RICHARD NORMAN STEVENSON
GEORGE HENRY JOHNSON
JOHN HARDY
P. HACKETT
GERALD HAMILTON
CARL STABLEFORD BRUXBY*

*6th December 1945

1946

ELSIE MAY GILMOUR*
MRS. M. A. INGLE*
CHARLES BENNETT
ARTHUR HORATIO DUDDELL
PERCY HACKETT
GEORGE C. LOWE
RALPH FOSTER KELSALL
HOWARD GEORGE PARSONS
RICHARD NORMAN STEVENSON
FRANCIS JOHN HARDY†
WILLIAM ERIC BIRD†

*First lady members of Council
†29th October 1948

27th May 1949

C. BENNETT
FRANCIS J. HARDY
ELSIE MAY GILMOUR
WILLIAM E. BIRD
RICHARD N. STEVENSON
H. G. PARSONS
GEORGE C. LOWE

The Parish Councils of 1894/95 and 1994/95

27th May 1949

JAMES GEORGE NEVILLE
RALPH FOSTER KELSALL*
KATHLEEN MARGARET MEE†

25th June 1949, †12th September 1951

25th May 1952

CHARLES BENNETT
DOROTHY DIXON
ELSIE MAY GILMOUR
FRANCIS JOHN HARDY
WILLIAM JOHN HOULT
GEORGE C. LOWE
KATHLEEN M. MEE
H. G. PARSONS
PHILIP H. POTTER

1955

DOROTHY DIXON
ELSIE M. GILMOUR
F. J. HARDY
HENRY JAMES
GEORGE C. LOWE
KATHLEEN M. MEE
H. G. PARSONS
P. H. POTTER
HUGH GARNER TAYLOR
REV. FRANK ANDERSON MOSS*
LT. COL. EDWARD LITTLER LOWE†

14th December 1956, †28th March 1957

28th May 1958

G. C. LOWE
ELSIE M. GILMOUR
H. G. PARSONS
P. H. POTTER
DOROTHY DIXON
HENRY JAMES
HUGH G. TAYLOR
REV F. A. MOSS
COL. E. L. LOWE

25th May 1961

COL. E. L. LOWE
GEORGE C. LOWE
ELSIE M. GILMOUR
DOROTHY DIXON
HOWARD G. PARSONS
P. H. POTTER
W. J. HOULT
KENNETH STANLEY GREEN
REV. F. A. MOSS§
HENRY JAMES*
ALBERT EDWARD GRETTON†
VICTOR PERCY HAIME†

§Elected but did not sign book
4th October 1961, †8th November 1961

1964

DOROTHY DIXON
ELSIE M. GILMOUR
K. S. GREEN§
V. P. HAIME
A. E. GRETTON
W. J. HOULT
ARTHUR LAURENCE JACKSON
HENRY JAMES*
COL. E. L. LOWE
H. G. PARSONS
P. H. POTTER

§Elected but did not sign book
30th July 1964

6th July 1967

Norman Edward Bailey
Robert Leslie Clucas*
Dorothy Dixon
E. M. Gilmour
K. S. Green
A. E. Gretton
V. P. Haime
W. J. Hoult
Col. E. L. Lowe
P. H. Potter
William Reginald Taylor

*25th May 1967

21st May 1970

N. E. Bailey
Gerald Edward Carey
Dorothy Dixon
E. M. Gilmour
K. S. Green
A. E. Gretton
V. P. Haime
Peter Henderson
W. J. Hoult
Col. E. L. Lowe
P. H. Potter
Robert L. Clucas*
Kathleen Mary Freeman†
Arthur William Seddon‡
Arthur Taylor Kennedy¶

*Co-opted 4th February 1971
†Co-opted 5th August 1971
‡Co-opted 14th December 1971
¶Co-opted 6th July 1972 after death of Col. Lowe

14th May 1973

N. E. Bailey
Ann Ball
May Ball
Ruth Mary Barker
Terence Edward Bond
Gerald Edward Carey
Dorothy Dixon
Elsie M. Gilmour
W. J. Hoult
P. H. Potter
Arthur W. Seddon
Arthur Taylor Kennedy*

*Co-opted 5th December 1974 after resignation Mrs Barker

13th May 1976

Douglas Brian Adderley
Anthoula Ball
May Ball
Hazel Mary Brindley
Gerald E. Carey 7C
Tom Stanley Deeming 7V & 8C
Dorothy Dixon
Godfrey John Patrick Eaton
P. H. Potter
Thomas Daniel Locke
Keith Frederick Pugh
Arthur Taylor Kennedy* & 8V

*Elected 9th December 1976 after resignation D. B. Adderley
7C Chairman & 7V Vice-Chairman 1977
8C Chairman & 8V Vice-Chairman 1978

The Parish Councils of 1894/95 and 1994/95

5th July 1979

Tom S. Deeming
John Ennor O'Brien
Pauline Diane Chandler
Norman Horton
John Stewart Dain
Godfrey J. P. Eaton
Arthur T. Kennedy
Anthoula Ball
Hazel Mary Brindley
Harry Matthews Stainburn
James Hogy Stewart
Stephen Sanderson*
Edward Millington Jones†

5th March 1981, †6th August 1981

13th May 1983

Michael Brookes
Rosemary Ellen de Leeta M. Eaton
Peter John Jepson
Jeffrey Pattison
Anthoula Ball
John Stewart Dain 3C
Tom S. Deeming
Norman Horton
E. Millington Jones
Arthur T. Kennedy
John E. O'Brien
John Charles Jay*

Elected 2nd August 1984 after resignation M. Brookes, 3C Chairman 1983

14th May 1987

Roger James Appleby
Anthoula Ball OC
John S. Dain
John C. Jay
Peter J. Jepson
Arthur T. Kennedy
Paula Ann Knight
Jeffrey Pattison 7C
William Eric Shingles
Ronald Walker George Tovey
Tom S. Deeming

7C *Chairman 1987, 1988 & 1989*
OC *Chairman 1990*

10th May 1991

Michael Charles Ackroyd
Anthoula Ball
T. S. Deeming
Linda Mary James
J. C. Jay
P. J. Jepson 2C
A. T. Kennedy 4C
J. Pattison 1C
Irene Susan Plant
William E. Shingles
Roy Smith
Robert Scattergood*

*Co-opted 3rd December 1992 after resignation Mrs Plant
1C *Chairman 1991*
2C *Chairman 1992 & 1993*
4C *Chairman 1994*

This completes 100 years of Parish Councillors. The minute book covering the first 30 years of the Parish Council is missing. One may assume that the Councillors of 1913 remained in office during the Great War, similar to the Councillors of 1937 during the Second World War. The first Parish Council Chairman was probably A. R. White. During 1902 to 1923 it may be assumed that the first signatory would be the Chairman for that term, but we are not sure of this fact. During the 1980's the Chairman signed every year as each new term began in May; this continues today.

It is interesting to note that before the Second World War, Parish Councillors were looked upon as being only "the gentry". According to one elderly lady in the 20's girls had to bob a curtsey and boys lift their cap if they met a councillor in the street.

Some families followed the tradition of being Parish Councillors: the Hardy's, J. A. Hoult and grandson W. J. Hoult, Thomas Dixon and his daughter-in-law Mrs. D. Dixon, the Lowe's, George and Edward, and two members of the Fowler-Butler family. Two vicars have been members, Rev. Fairclough and Rev. Moss, and three doctors, Dr. Palmer, Dr. T. Dixon and Dr. Taylor.

Since Miss Gilmour and Mrs. M. A. Ingle paved the way for ladies in 1946, only another 12 have followed their example.

CHAIRMEN OF BARTON-UNDER-NEEDWOOD PARISH COUNCIL

1894/06		1911/12	
1896/07	ARTHUR ROBSON WHITE	1912/13	
1897/08	ARTHUR ROBSON WHITE	1913/14	
1898/09	ARTHUR ROBSON WHITE	1914/15	
1899/00	JOSEPH DOVE	1915/16	
1900/01	JOSEPH DOVE	1916/17	
1901/02	ROBERT HENRY FOWLER BUTLER	1917/18	
1902/03		1918/19	
1903/04		1919/20	
1904/05		1920/21	
1905/06		1921/22	
1906/07		1922/23	
1907/08		1923/24	
1908/09		1924/25	HENRY GUY NADIN
1909/10		1925/26	HENRY GUY NADIN
1910/11		1926/27	HENRY GUY NADIN

The Parish Councils of 1894/95 and 1994/95

1927/28	HENRY GUY NADIN	1961/62	LT COL EDWARD LITTLER LOWE
1928/29	HENRY GUY NADIN	1962/63	LT COL EDWARD LITTLER LOWE
1929/30	HENRY GUY NADIN	1963/64	LT COL EDWARD LITTLER LOWE
1930/31	HENRY GUY NADIN	1964/65	LT COL EDWARD LITTLER LOWE
1931/32	HENRY GUY NADIN	1965/66	LT COL EDWARD LITTLER LOWE
1932/33	HENRY GUY NADIN	1966/67	PHILIP H POTTER
1933/34	HENRY GUY NADIN	1967/68	PHILIP H POTTER
1934/35	HENRY GUY NADIN/ F W HARDY	1968/69	ELSIE MAY GILMOUR
		1969/70	ELSIE MAY GILMOUR
1935/36	THOMAS STANLEY GREEN	1970/71	WILLIAM JOHN HOULT
1936/37	THOMAS STANLEY GREEN	1971/72	WILLIAM JOHN HOULT
1937/38	THOMAS STANLEY GREEN	1972/73	NORMAN EDWARD BAILEY
1938/39	THOMAS STANLEY GREEN	1973/74	NORMAN EDWARD BAILEY
1939/40	GEORGE HENRY JOHNSON	1974/75	ELSIE MAY GILMOUR
1940/41	GEORGE HENRY JOHNSON	1975/76	ELSIE MAY GILMOUR
1941/42	GEORGE HENRY JOHNSON	1976/77	THOMAS DANIEL LOCKE/ ANN BALL
1942/43	GEORGE HENRY JOHNSON		
1943/44	GEORGE HENRY JOHNSON	1977/78	GERALD E CAREY
1944/45	GEORGE HENRY JOHNSON	1978/79	TOM STANLEY DEEMING
1945/46	GEORGE HENRY JOHNSON	1979/80	ARTHUR TAYLOR KENNEDY
1946/47	GEORGE CECIL LOWE	1980/81	ARTHUR TAYLOR KENNEDY
1947/48	GEORGE CECIL LOWE	1981/82	JOHN STEWART DAIN
1948/49	GEORGE CECIL LOWE	1982/83	JOHN STEWART DAIN
1949/50	GEORGE CECIL LOWE	1983/84	JOHN STEWART DAIN
1950/51	GEORGE CECIL LOWE	1984/85	ARTHUR TAYLOR KENNEDY
1951/52	GEORGE CECIL LOWE	1985/86	NORMAN HORTON
1952/53	GEORGE CECIL LOWE	1986/87	EDWARD MILLINGTON JONES
1953/54	GEORGE CECIL LOWE	1987/88	JEFFREY PATTISON
1954/55	GEORGE CECIL LOWE	1988/89	JEFFREY PATTISON
1955/56	GEORGE CECIL LOWE	1989/90	JEFFREY PATTISON
1956/57	GEORGE CECIL LOWE	1990/91	ANN BALL/PETER J JEPSON
1957/58	GEORGE CECIL LOWE	1991/92	JEFFREY PATTISON
1958/59	GEORGE CECIL LOWE	1992/93	PETER JOHN JEPSON
1959/60	GEORGE CECIL LOWE	1993/94	PETER JOHN JEPSON
1960/61	LT COL EDWARD LITTLER LOWE	1994/95	ARTHUR TAYLOR KENNEDY

Barton Parish Council 1994/1995

At the elections of 1991, when the present council was voted in, only eleven candidates, stood for the eleven places, which meant there was no need for a public election. Councillors do all their work voluntarily; the only paid servant of the village is the Parish Clerk, who takes minutes at meetings and deals with correspondence. The councillors, besides attending monthly meetings, also attend sub-committees to deal with such things as planning, the fish pond, the allotments and whatever crops up. The time spent by each councillor on parish business can be anything from an hour or two each month, to several hours per week, all done out of their desire to help care for the village and its people.

Of the eleven councillors all are still in office except Mrs. S. Plant who resigned in 1992, when Mr. R. Scattergood was co-opted as the only candidate putting his name forward. The present council's term of office ends on May 5th 1995, when, if more than eleven names are submitted, an election will take place. At the time of writing (February 1995) two councillors have indicated that they will not be standing.

The "centenary" councillor's names are listed here in similar style to the first council. Very little seems to change in 100 years. People put down their roots in the village and then take an active part in the decisions affecting Barton. No doubt this pattern will continue.

Arthur Taylor Kennedy (Chairman 1994/95)

Born 1937 in Glasgow, brought up from the age of two years in Birmingham. Arthur moved to Barton in 1965; he is married with two sons and has been a parish councillor since 1972. Arthur has been chairman of the Civic Society since 1981, chairman of the Barton Neighbourhood Watch since 1985, and has been chairman of the Best Kept Village committee and the parish council. Arthur is a self employed builder.

William Eric Shingles (Vice-Chairman 1994/95)

Born 1923 in Edgbaston, Birmingham and moved to Barton in 1967. Bill is married with three sons, and has been a parish councillor since 1987. He is a retired engineer, and states that one of the most interesting commissions of his business was the designing and building of a gun which was used in the film of Frederick Forsyth's book *Day of the Jackal*, which involved meeting the author, director and actors on the film set.

The Parish Councils of 1894/95 and 1994/95

PETER JOHN JEPSON

Born 1931 in Manchester, Peter has lived in the area for over fifty years, residing in Barton village since 1970. He is married with two daughters and one son, and has been a parish councillor since 1983. He is secretary of the village hall management committee, and has been parish council chairman. Peter is a retired heat transfer engineer.

JEFFREY PATTISON

Born 1943 at Bishop Auckland, and moved to Barton in 1970. Jeff is married with two daughters and one son and has been a parish councillor since 1983. He has been chairman of the parish council, is chairman of the Centenary committee, treasurer of the village hall management committee and vice-chairman of the Royal British Legion. Jeff is a retired British Coal Board worker.

TOM STANLEY DEEMING

Born 1917 in Birmingham and moved to Barton in 1967. Married with three sons Stan has been a parish councillor since 1976. He is also an East Staffs Borough councillor, a past chairman of that same council as well as a past chairman of the Barton parish council. Stan is a retired British Coal Board marketing manager.

ANTHOULA BALL

Born 1926 in Athens Greece and moved to Barton in 1970 married with two daughters and one son. Anne has been a parish councillor since 1973 is a past chairwoman of the council and currently an East Staffs Borough councillor.

JOHN C. JAY

Born 1927 in Rugby Warwickshire and moved to Barton in 1966. John is married and is a retired wages cost clerk. He has been a parish councillor since 1984.

LINDA M. JAMES

Born 1944 in Hammersmith London and moved to Barton in 1979. Linda has been a parish councillor since 1991 and she represents the council on the school governors board for the Thomas Russell Primary School. Linda is a social worker.

Michael C. Ackroyd

Born 1951 in Bradford Yorkshire and moved to Barton in 1985. Mike is married with one daughter and one son. He has been a councillor since 1991 and is an area sales engineer.

Roy H. D. Smith

Born 1941 in Middlesex, and moved to Barton in 1985 he is married with one daughter and two sons. Roy has been a parish councillor since 1991 and he is a railway accountant.

Robert Scattergood

Born in 1947 at Burton-on-Trent and moved to Barton in 1948. Bob is married with one daughter and two sons. He is Chairman of the Holland Sports Club has been a councillor since 1992 and is self-employed.

The Clerk to the Parish Council:
Michelle Saddington

Born in Birmingham moved to Barton in 1988. Michelle is married with one daughter.

Chapter Eight

BARTON TODAY

DURING the 20th century the village has witnessed a number of major housing developments and much in-filling among the older buildings on Main Street and elsewhere. There has been a threefold increase in population from the 1881 census figure of 1,789. The education facilities expanded to meet this extra demand with the building of the Secondary School in 1958, and the Junior School in 1968.

The latter half of the century has seen the demise of the importance of the railways. The Barton & Walton railway station, built in 1840, operated until 1957 when it was closed to passenger traffic and has since been demolished. The car has become the mode of transport of the masses. A major trunk road, the A38 dual carriageway, which passes to the east of the village, follows the route of the Roman road, Ryknield Street, along the middle of the Trent valley. Two major intersections have been built to gain access to the village from the A38. The one at Barton Turn passes over the Trent and Mersey Canal near to Wharf House and its canal lock and spans the A38 beside the site of the Barton & Walton railway station. The other spans the canal and A38 just south of Catholme at Dogshead Lane. A marina is being built beside the Trent and Mersey Canal at Barton Turn.

The Main Street is endowed with the historical legacy of the village for it accommodates a number of old dwellings and buildings. The 19th-century entrepreneur Sam Coulson's bricks were used to clad the shops and cottages concealing their beamed Tudor origins. In the neighbourhood of the village are several handsome old villa residences, Barton Hall, Nuttall House, Holly Hurst, Silver Hill, Fulbrook House and The Knoll.

The three village schools cater for infant, junior and secondary pupils. The Infant and Junior Schools retain the name of Thomas Russell, the London Draper who established the endowed free grammar school in 1593, which was replaced in 1885. The John Taylor High School, which bears the name of the most famous of the 16th century triplets, is a large secondary school with a catchment area covering the surrounding villages to the south west of Burton on Trent. There are a number of nursery and play groups catering for the pre-school children. This wealth of education establishments is complemented by a youth club, a library, and an adult education centre. The needs of the community are also served by the St James' Church Hall, in St James' Road, and the Village Hall, in Crowberry Lane. The Village Hall, built in 1988, replaced the old Central Hall which had served the village since the 19th century. The Roman Catholic and Methodist Churches have small meeting rooms which are also used by the community.

Direct links between the Thomas Russell School and the Drapers' Company of London were severed in the late 19th century. But the links were renewed in 1993, when the Drapers' Company visited the village to commemorate the quatercentenary of the death of Thomas Russell and the founding of his school. They unveiled a plaque on the Thomas Russell Infant School and have endowed an annual bursary of £100 to the three schools of the village.

The religious needs of the village are catered for by churches of four denominations. Those of the Protestant Church of England faith attend the Tudor St. James' Church in the Main Street, built by John Taylor in 1517. Those of the Roman Catholic faith attend the Church in Wales Lane. While the Methodists attend their Church in Crowberry Lane, established in 1828, and the Christadelphians attend in their Church, converted in the late 1970's from farm buildings, in upper Main Street. The Mission Church at Barton Turns has been converted into offices and the Wesleyan Chapel in Wales Lane was demolished about 1980 to make way for housing for senior citizens (Radhurst Rise).

There is a Health Centre in Short Lane manned by four doctors and incorporating a Health Clinic and Health Visitor service. Also in Short Lane is the Cottage Hospital, built in 1879, with the main hospital for the area situated in Burton on Trent. There is a private nursing home at the Towers in Dunstall Road. The elderly are catered for by the Mayflower Club and a Meals on Wheels Service. To complete the needs of the sick there are a Chemist and a Dentist in Main Street.

There are a number of shops in the village, predominantly in Main Street with a small shopping mall at Oak Road. The variety of shops and facilities available are Antiques, Bank, Barbers, Beauty Care Clinic, Books, Butchers, Car repairs, Chemist, Chinese Take-away, Estate Agents, Fish & Chips, Fishing tackle, Furniture, Florists, Grocery stores, Hairdressers, Newsagent, Pet food, Post Office, Stationery, Supermarket, Veterinary Surgeon and Wines & Spirits. Those wishing to imbibe the delights of the breweries of Burton-on-Trent have a wide choice of venues. Beside the Holland Sports and the Barton Bowls Clubs there are seven public houses: the Barton

Turn, the Three Horse Shoes, the Shoulder of Mutton, the Middle Bell, the Red Lion, the Royal Oak and the Top Bell at Barton Gate.

The village culture is endowed with several active societies which make full use of the Village and Church Halls and meeting rooms as well as the John Taylor school. Barton Players, Barton Wind Bands, British Red Cross, Choral societies, Civic Society, Flower Club, Gardening Guild, Guides & Brownies, Model Engineering Society, Mothers' Union, Neighbourhood Watch, Royal British Legion, Scouts & Cubs and Women's Institute to name but a few.

Leisure time is also enriched with an abundance of sporting facilities at the Holland Sports Club, the Barton Bowls Club, the two halls and schools. The sports available to the village are Badminton, Cricket, Crown Green Bowling, Football, Hockey, Karate, Netball, Rugby, Table Tennis, Tennis and Tug of War, while the Angling fraternity have a choice of fishing on the village pond, the Trent & Mersey canal or the River Trent. There are two allotment areas for those wanting to expand their horticultural skills.

There are a number of yearly events occurring in the village, the more notable ones being the Shrovetide pancake race in February, the Holland Sports Club Gala in June, the open gardens weekend in July, the village Horticultural show in September, and the Cubs and Scouts Guy Fawkes bonfire in November.

The beneficence of William Key is still carried out today under the auspices of the trustees for the Henry Warford and William Key Charities. The income of the William Key charity is raised by renting the land at Bonthorne, the allotments opposite Bonthorne Farm in Dogshead Lane and the adjacent field known as Bonthorne Common; and the land at Lincroft, the field adjacent to A38 on the area known as Fatholme between Barton Turn and Catholme. One of the conditions of the charity, which is still carried out today, is that the vicar, at present the Reverend Tony Wood, still preaches a sermon on Good Friday for which he is paid the sum of 50 pence (ten shillings) by the charity. All the other charities of Barton-under-Needwood were amalgamated into the Eleemosynary Charities in 1902 for administration and are managed by a body of trustees. They still continue today to serve the needy of the village, the net income being given to the poor and elderly of the village at Christmas by the Trustees.

The income from the land bequeathed by William Key in 1651 at Bonthorne and Lincroft was to be put to charitable use for the good of the poor of Barton-under-Needwood and Dunstall. The gross income of the William Key Charity in November 1994 was £461; after the deduction of expenses the residue was divided between Dunstall 20%, St James' Church 20% and the Eleemosynary Charities 60%.

Under the Needwood Tree

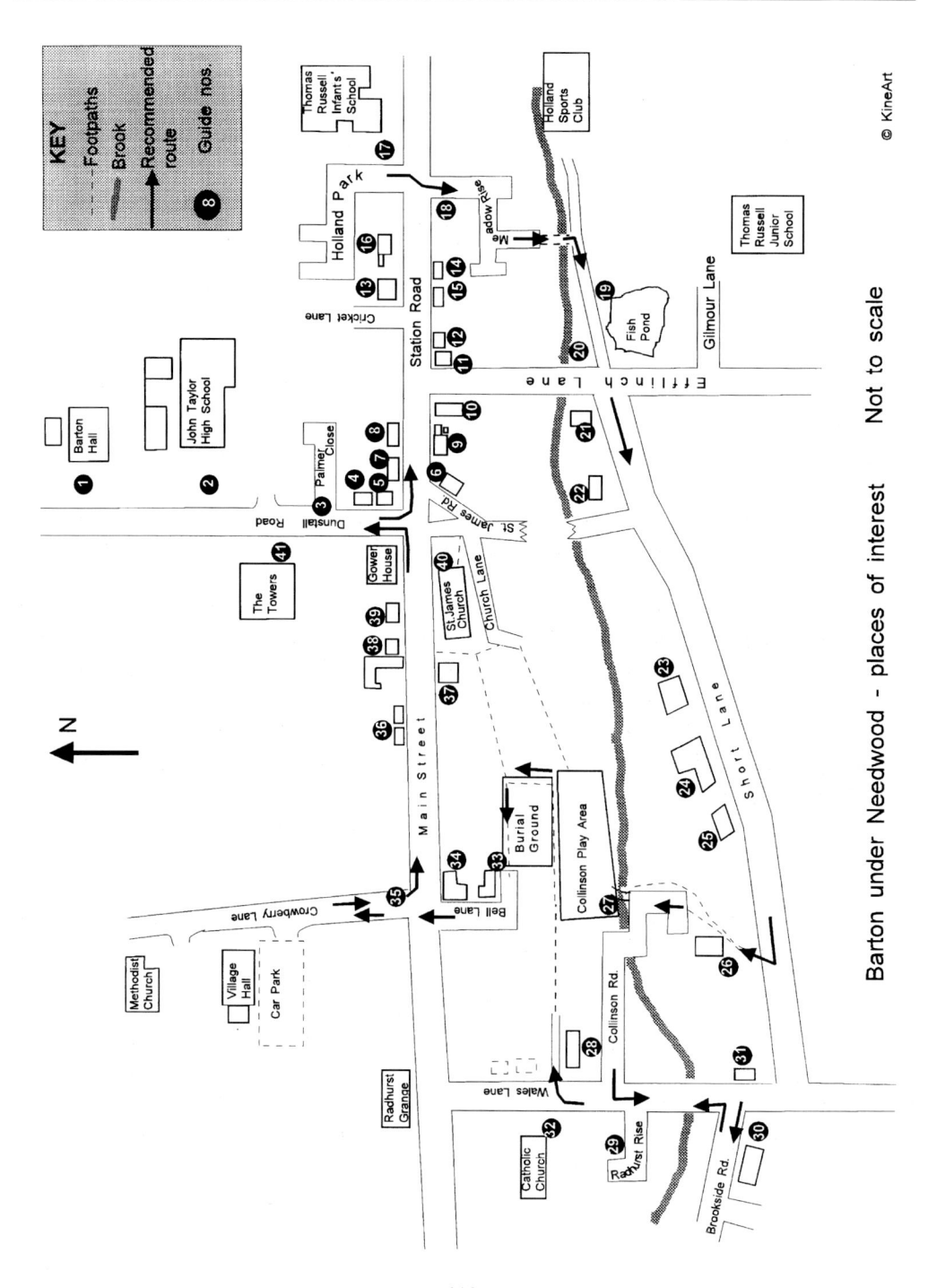

Barton under Needwood - places of interest

Chapter Nine

A Walk Around Barton

IF you have enjoyed reading about the history of the village, you may well like to have a walk around the route that follows, and discover the actual historical properties that still survive today.

This walk was initially organised by the Barton Civic Society in 1984 for a visit by Derby Civic Society members, then updated in 1994 as a 90-minute evening walk at the request of Barton Library to encourage people to be aware of the history and beauty of the areas they live in. This proved most successful with over 50 people taking advantage of a fine May evening. Members of the Civic Society acted as guides taking copies of the guide notes, which give just a brief flavour of the architecture and history, updated again for inclusion in this book to include more properties and information en route. We hope you enjoy a pleasant stroll and bring alive once more some of the characters and events you have read about in this book. We also hope it has not changed too much in years to come.

CHRISTINE and ARTHUR KENNEDY
February 1995

We start the walk in Dunstall Road, once known as Nottle or Nuttall End. The first major building of note is Barton Hall (1) said to have been built in 1724 – no evidence is available but is probably from a date stone. In Shaw's *Staffordshire* of 1798 it is described thus: "On the North side of the village stands Barton Hall, a good modern mansion with suitable offices, etc. The property of Mrs Butler". By the 1830's it belonged to the Fowler-Butler family and in 1839 the owner and occupier was Richard Fowler-Butler. Robert Henry Fowler-Butler was the owner in 1900 and was a Parish Councillor from 1901 to 1913. Colonel Richard Fowler-Butler is listed as a Councillor in 1920. No owner is listed in the Directories of 1928 and 1936 which suggests it was empty.

Under the Needwood Tree

The building was modernised, retaining it's character in 1978, by the then owner Mr. S. W. Clarke, who presently resides at the Knoll. During the modernisation of the separate building known as the Deer House (origionally thought to have been built as a coach house, grain store and grooms quarters) lead flashing was discovered to have the names of the workmen who rebuilt it inscribed in it: S. Barlow, joiner and James Ludlow, plumber — dated May 1873. It is not known why it was titled the "Deer House" but it was possibly used as a hunting lodge for the nearby Needwood Forest and indeed a small collection of antlers was found in the building.

We continue along Dunstall Road and pause outside the gateway to the John Taylor High School on your left (2). Built in 1958 with extensions costing £200,000 it went comprehensive in September 1972. Named after the illustrious John Taylor you have read about in an earlier chapter of the book, the school is built on what in past years had been a piece of sporting history. Barton was one of the first places in the provinces to take to polo. It had its own polo field and also a golf course; both these, and further down the piece of land a cricket pitch, were on the site of the school. When the school was built, the Holland family gave the piece of land near the village pond to be the new cricket pitch. The land leading to the old pitch from Station Road and now ending on the boundary of the school playing field is known locally as Cricket Lane. The Golf Club was formed in 1892 with only 19 members. In a year this increased to 48 and boomed to 60 in 1894, but in 1895 the opening of a club in Burton took away members.

On to the first road which is Palmer Close (3) which leads to bungalows for elderly persons. The close is named after the Palmer family, particularly Dr Clement Palmer who was the village doctor and one of the first Parish Councillors in 1894/5. The family lived in Gower House on the opposite corner, using the room nearest the road junction for the surgery. The misses Palmer, Dr Palmer's daughters, lived here at Yew Trees (4) until their deaths. One sister married Colonel Lowe who was a prominent citizen and a Parish Councillor for many years. Dr Clement's son, Dr Ambrose Palmer was killed in the First World War. In the 1881 census it is recorded that Dr Palmer was then 37 years old and lived with his wife, seven children and five servants. Yew Tree Cottage was built in 1770. In the mid 1800s it was the home of the family "Garnet-Taylor" who were descendants of John Taylor.

The 'Shoulder of Mutton' (5) is a late 18th century grade two listed building, much altered. Note the Domesday plaque 1086-1986, acknowledging that Barton was named in the famous *Domesday Book*. The adjoining cottages are late 16th century, and were for 300 years, a saddlery.

The Old Vicarage (6) opposite and facing the Church is an early 19th Century Grade 2 listed building. The home in 1881 and for many years of Rev. Fairclough who

A Walk Around Barton

then according to the Census lived there with his wife, a boarder and four servants. The house was much bigger then; the rear which was the servants' quarters has been removed, leaving just the front half of the house.

No. 8 Main Street (7) is 18th Century and also Grade 2 listed.

Peel Cottage (8) was the first Police Station and also the jail from 1902 to 1964. Named, of course, after Robert Peel, founder of the Police Force. When the Police acquired the property it was a thatched cottage with wattle and daub walls. They had it bricked up and tiled the roof to replace the thatch. It was built by a builder called Mr Ball, whose grand-daughter lives only a few yards away today.

The White House (9) opposite is a 17th Century building with 19th Century alterations. It is Grade 2 listed. In the 1960's and 70's a colourful lady ran an antique shop in the house. She also made so-called "love potions" which went all round the world, even being sold in Harrods! A letter was received addressed to the "Mayor of Barton" from Germany, and upon translation proved to be another request for supplies!

The building on the corner of Efflinch Lane was once the old Blacksmiths Shop (10). The 1881 census gives Simon Spence as Landlord of the Three Horseshoes and also a blacksmith; we therefore assume that this was his workshop, as on the opposite corner stands the Inn (11), which is a 16th Century coaching Inn, with magnificent beam work still preserved as a feature in both bar and lounge. Looking at the profile of the Inn on Efflinch Lane, you will see the small cottage which was No. 3 Efflinch Lane, now part of the Inn. It used to house a cobbler's shop. No. 5 Efflinch Lane was demolished to make the Inn car park.

Barton Court (12) now re-named Barton House was built c.1840 and is Grade 2 listed. In 1881 it was the home of Woodforde F. Woodforde who was a County Court Judge, and later became the home of Arthur Robson White, J.P. one of the first Parish Councillors.

Red Cross HQ (13). This used to be a shop run by a lady called Miss Durant, and was known as "Miss Durant's Fancy Repository". It was owned by Miss Holland who gave it to the Red Cross in 1958; it has been refurbished in 1994/95 by public donations and fundraising. Opposite (14) No. 22 Station Road was a sweet shop owned by Mrs Howard where children called on their way to school. Miss Holland also bought this property. No. 20, the cottage called "Wyatts", was named after a Victorian architect of some note.

Castle House (16) was called "The Grove" until recently and was built in 1730. It is now divided into three dwellings, but was once the home of Miss Mary Holland who was a suffragette in the early 1900s.

Thomas Russell Infant School (17). Built in 1855 near the site of the original Elizabethan school. Note the plaque presented by the Drapers' Company in 1993 to commemorate the 400th anniversary of the death of Thomas Russell.

Under the Needwood Tree

Meadow Rise (18), built in the late 1960's on the site of a large property, Holland House, seat of the Hollands of Barton. Richard de Holland was the first to settle in Barton in 1314 and there were Hollands in Barton for over 600 years, probably a record for any family! The Victorian Hollands were benefactors of the village; it is reputed they were friends of W. G. Grace, the cricketer, who visited them at Holland House. The family also gave the village sports ground now known as Holland Sports Club.

Walk through Meadow Rise and you come to a footbridge over the brook which leads you to the Fishpond, one of the most attractive spots in the village. This is shown on maps as early as 1800 and in Victorian times had a drive all around it suitable for horse-drawn vehicles. Across the pond, between the trees you can see the Thomas Russell Junior School, built in 1968 to take the growing number of children from the Infant School. At the end of the drive is the Sports Club, home to many sports activities as diverse as tug of war and tennis, cricket and hockey and of course football of both rugby and soccer versions.

Cross Efflinch Lane (20), once known as Walkers Lane after the family of the famous "Johnny Walker Whisky" who once lived in Barton; it is one of the oldest roads in the village. The name Efflinch is derived from 'Haiflinch' which is a Saxon word meaning 'heather on marshy ground'. The lane to the Junior School was named in honour of Miss Elsie May Gilmour who was for many years active in Parish Council, W.I., Red Cross and many other organisations, a lady much respected and liked by all who knew her.

After crossing Efflinch Lane we enter Short Lane, originally Wilkes Lane and locally known as Hospital Lane (for reasons which will become clear further up the lane). The first building we come to is without doubt one of Barton's oldest surviving properties (21), built as two cottages in about 1560, converted to one by the present owner in 1948 when the exterior was cement-rendered and a new slate roof put on. Old records say there were three cottages on this site but no trace has been found of foundations over the past 50 years. It is also thought that the cottages were attached to No. 6 and may have been farm buildings. The original timbers are still there to be seen and in very good condition. In the 15th and 16th centuries it was common practice to build properties "end on" to roads, lanes or tracks. En route along Short Lane we pass two large family semi-detached villas built in 1896 on what was a deep hollow in the land. This was filled up so that building work could be carried out.

Crossing St James Road we come to Barton Fire Station (23). Built in 1965 it has twelve retained part-time firemen on call. Note the memorial garden and seat to the memory of a fireman who died in a car accident on the A38.

A Walk Around Barton

Barton Hall, Dunstall Road
Built in 1724, it was occupied at the turn of the century by Lieut. Col. Fowler-Butler, J.P.

Nuttall House, Dunstall Road
One-time seat of the Sanders family. The house name was instrumental in the area being called 'Nottle End' in Victorian times. It came from Nuttall End — Nottle End

Under the Needwood Tree

Silverhill, off Barton Gate
One-time home of the Lyons family, owners of Barton Gas Company

Wales End Farm, Wales Lane
A 15th century building; the oldest part of the building, the hall, is dated from 1450, possibly the oldest building in Barton

Barton Cottage Hospital (24) was built in 1879 by William Sharpe who was a well-known local builder; his picture hangs in the Hall of the hospital to this day. It is well used by patients for respite and convalescent care and is always on hand to treat small accidents, cuts and bruises when the doctors' surgery is closed. In the early days the village Doctor used to perform operations here as well.

Barton Health Centre (25) was built in the mid 1970's and is home to three full-time and one part-time doctor, practice nurses and many other facilities.

Follow the footpath leading from the "kissing gate" and you reach The Manor (26) once an inn or coaching stop called "The Hit and Miss" because it wasn't easy to find and you either "hit it or missed it"! It was built c1600 and is Grade 2 listed. Continue alongside the house by the footpath and you reach Collinson Road — in front of you is the children's play area which was once known as "Collinson Croft". The ground was purchased by the Parish Council in 1954 with the remains of the money collected for celebrating the Coronation of Queen Elizabeth II. The cost was £250 and the remainder of the sum was made up by public subscription.

Coming out of Collinson Road into Wales Lane on your right is the site of the workhouse and the alms houses; these are now an 'L' shaped cottage (28). On the same spot the "lock up" — forerunner of the jail and the site of the original fire station which was in existence at least as far back as 1820 with a horse-drawn engine.

Opposite, where now there stands Radhurst Rise (29) once stood a Primitive Wesleyan Chapel built in 1842 and demolished in the late 1960's.

Walk up Wales Lane (turning left from Collinson Road) and you reach Brookside Road. Just along on the left is Wales End Farm (30). 14th Century and Grade 2 listed, it was once owned by a Johannes Holand de Walesend in 1509, one of the Holland family (the name was spelt either way during the centuries). Return to Wales Lane and cross to the cottage called Barn Cottage (31). This was originally a late medieval cruck building of five bays; this means that the roof is made of tall curving timbers meeting at the apex of the roof.

Return to the site of the alms houses — look across the road and you will see the Church of Our Lady which is Barton's Catholic Church (32) and was built in 1963.

Take the footpath which is alongside the "almshouses" cottage and it leads back into the play area, turn left into the burial ground and go left through the gates into Bell Lane (33), originally called Fitchett Lane. This leads into Main Street and has the Middle Bell (34) on the right, which was originally two cottages, late 18th century and Grade 2 listed.

Barton used to have many more inns and ale houses, besides the seven which still exist: The Bell, The Royal Oak, The Three Horseshoes, The Shoulder of Mutton, The Red Lion, The "Top" Bell at Barton Gate and the Barton Turns (formerly The Vine).

Under the Needwood Tree

There have been names such as "The Snake with Two Heads" in Wales Lane, "The Manchester Arms" also in Wales Lane, "The Robin Hood" in Main Street (opposite what is now Park Road), "The Railway Inn" at Barton Turns, "The Three Crowns" at Barton Turns, "The Junction Inn" in Efflinch Lane, "The Flitch of Bacon" on the A38 and "The White Swan" opposite the Church, and all these to serve a population a fifth the size of today's!

Opposite Bell Lane is Crowberry Lane. At the top of Crowberry Lane stand two very contrasting buildings: the Village Hall built in 1988 after the old Central Hall which had stood on the site since the mid 1800s became unsafe and had to be demolished, and the Methodist Church which was built in 1828.

Returning to Main Street turn left at Crowberry Lane's end and walk towards St James' Church. The shops and cottages in Main Street (once called Penny Lane) were black and white timber and thatch in Tudor style, but in the early 1800s a landlord of the Shoulder of Mutton, one Samuel Coulson, was also the owner of a brickyard and talked the residents into bricking up the fronts of the buildings. If you look between the shops, just past the hairdresser's, there is a gap too small to be reached where the timbers are still visible (36).

The Old Parsonage (37) on the right near the Church was once a coaching station, the site of a parsonage (before the Old Vicarage), site also of the Post Office once kept by the Misses Holland, and also later in the 1970's/80's a Post Office again. Modernised in the last few years, five houses were built in what was an extensive garden. During excavations to build the houses, Roman artefacts were found, including coins.

The building which is now an Estate Agent's was once "The White Swan Inn" (38). The 17th Century timber-framed cottage (39) next door is reputed to have been the site of the home of John Taylor, who built St James' Church (40), which you should now visit. You will find it a most interesting experience.

On the corner of Dunstall Road we reach Gower House again and beyond it stands "The Towers" residential home (41) which was once called Nuttall House. Nuttall was often called "Chimney Pot Hall" by villagers and once was the home of a Miss Nadin who owned the first gramophone in the village and two records which were put to much use at dances in the Central Hall.

You have now completed a circle and we hope you have enjoyed your walk and will remember it with pleasure.

Some other notable buildings of Barton, not on the planned route of the "Walk" but worthy of mention.

Radhurst Grange, on Main Street opposite Wales Lane junction. It was built about 1760, and was probably part of the Dunstall Estate owned by one of the famous

A Walk Around Barton

Arkwright Brothers, mill-owners of Derbyshire, who lived at Dunstall Hall. In a sale brochure of 1851 the house is listed as having a surgery and consulting rooms; from 1841 to 1868 the owner was a surgeon named Thomas Webb. In 1881 Joseph Holdsworth lived there with his wife, sister, six children and one servant, plus seven boys aged between 12 and 15 years who were boarding scholars. Indeed Mr. Holdsworth ran the house as a boarding school. In the 1940's and 50's a corn merchant lived at the house, and was apt to over-imbibe at the Golden Cup public house in Yoxall. Fortunately his horse knew the way home, and was used to finding its own way, always delivering master and cart safely.

Opposite Radhurst Grange, in Wales Lane stands Three Ways Cottage. This was once known as Penny Hill Mansion; the top end of Wales Lane was known as Penny Hill. This cottage has had a varied existence, once as a thriving corner shop, fish and chip shop, grocer's shop, antiques shop, wool shop and at present a bed and breakfast accommodation.

Along Main Street, towards Barton Gate, on the right hand side, at the end of a tree-lined drive stands The Knoll. The older building built by Sir Robert Peel has long since been demolished, but on its site stands the present building, built in 1884 by John Reed Walker, J.P. of whisky fame. The rear part of this wonderful building was re-built after a fire in 1894. Miss Beatrice Emily Nadin, who married Mr. J. A. White at St. James's church in 1899, was given away by her brother H. G. Nadin of the Knoll. In the 1960's it was owned by the Roman Catholic Church who used it as a training school for young priests.

Along Barton Gate, on the right hand side, standing way back, up a long drive is Silverhill. It was built in the 18th century but had major renovation work done in 1820, by Giles Scott, one of the most famous architects in the country, just before he carried out restoration work on Lichfield Cathedral. Many of the arches, windows and exterior wall motif's are identical but on a smaller scale to some in Lichfield Cathedral. It was owned by the Lyons family at one time, who were also the owners of Barton's gas works, and the present owner found more gas-pipes than water-pipes when he moved in. The last Lyons to live there were the two Miss Lyons. After them were Colonel and Lady Ritchie, sister to Mr. Harrison of Wychnor Hall, a big hunting family.

Along Efflinch Lane, opposite the junction with Arden Road, stands a row of Victorian cottages, known as White's Row. Presumably the owner was a Mr. White; there were a few prominent local owners of that name. They were the only buildings on the road in their day; people travelling from Wychnor or Alrewas to Barton, called them "halfway houses". Many years ago the eccentric character, Paddy Lindop, lived in the Wychnor end cottage.

Under the Needwood Tree

Further along the Efflinch we come to Captain's Lane, originally known as Greenhill Lane, and renamed in honour of Captain Arden who lived in Fullbrook House, the imposing building on the left hand side, as you walk up Captain's Lane.

Captain Arden was a descendant of the family of Mary Arden mother to William Shakespeare. On early maps the house is shown as Foo Brook (1834) foo being an old Scottish pronunciation for the word full hence Fullbrook House.

Down at Barton Turns stands the 18th-century Wharf House. The canal originally ended there and barges turned around in a basin. The area was very busy in the heyday of canal transport. Goods were loaded and unloaded at the Wharf House which was a staging post, being close to Ryknield Street. It was called the Three Crowns public house and provided accommodation for many years. It became a quiet backwater when the A38 was moved and widened in the late 1950's.

Postscript

WHEN the idea for a book to mark the Centenary Year of the Parish Council was first promoted, it was obvious that there was a need for someone with the time and expertise to listen to residents memories of Barton and record them. The person who came to mind was ex-policeman, and amateur local historian, Steve Gardner. Not a native of Barton, but having had an association with the village since 1975, and living in the village since 1983, Steve was Barton's Community Police Officer for eleven years, before retiring from the force after twenty years, through injury. Whilst at Barton Steve ran the Barton Police Community Scheme, a summer activity programme for children which was the forerunner to the county wide scheme. Steve was the Police liaison Officer on the Barton Neighbourhood Watch, from its start in 1985, and was Schools' Officer, teaching Police input lessons in the three village schools.

A keen sportsman, Steve has competed in amateur Weightlifting for many years, representing Great Britain, from 87 to 91 in Powerlifting, winning the 1990 European Heavyweight title in Belgium, and Silver Medal in the World Championships that same year in France. In the sport of All Round Weightlifting Steve won the World Heavyweight title in 1987 in Leicester, and in 1991 in Philadelphia U.S.A. Steve has been Captain and Coach of the Holland Tug of War Club since 1978, having joined them in 1975. The team's name "Holland" comes from the historic family that lived at Barton for 600 years, and who donated the land that the sports club stands on today. Steve has guided the village team to two national titles, being National Heavyweight champions, with the Tug of War Federation of Great Britain in 1989 and 1991, and also to two National inter-counties titles in 1991 and 1992, (not bad for a village team). The Holland Tug of War team celebrate twenty-five years of competition in this Centenary year.

Working on the book fired Steve with an ambition to become a Parish Councillor, and in the elections of May 1995 he was elected to serve on Barton Parish Council, together with four other new councillors; Adrian Wedgwood, Alison Wood, Pauline Fisher and Susan Walker. Countless hours of research and re-typing by Steve have gone into bringing this work to completion, but like 'Topsy' it has grown to become, we hope, an asset to those who have a thirst for the history of one of Staffordshire's most pleasant villages. No doubt many memories will be stirred, and perhaps brought forward to be added to those in the book, who knows? maybe enough for a second volume one day.

ARTHUR and CHRISTINE KENNEDY

Bibliography

R. Plot   *A History of Staffordshire* (1686)

S. Shaw   *History and Antiquities of Staffordshire* (1798)

Parson and Bradshaw   *Staffordshire General and Commercial Directory* (1818)

The Charities Commission Report for Barton-under-Needwood (1831)

White's History, Gazetteer and Directory of Staffordshire (1834 & 1851)

Pigot's Directory of Staffordshire (1835)

Kelly's Post Office Directory of Staffordshire (1860, 1864, 1872, 1880, 1896, 1940)

W. R. Holland   *Some Records of the Holland Family* (1929)

Alison Wood   *A Short History of John Taylor* (1981)
Alison Wood   *A Guide to the Parish Church of Barton-under-Needwood* (1981)

Barton History Group   *Barton in the 18th Century* (1983)
Barton History Group   *Barton-under-Needwood in 1881* (1983)

G. L. King   *The Printed Maps of Staffordshire 1577-1850* (2nd revised edition 1988)

G. E. Carey   *The Birmingham and Derby Junction Railway* (1989)
G. E. Carey   *A History of Thomas Russell and Barton School* (5th revised edition 1993)